M000086484

Coaching
with ECERS

Strategies and Tools to Improve
Quality in Pre-K & K Classrooms

Holly Seplocha

Foreword by Debby Cryer, Richard M. Clifford,
Thelma Harms, and Noreen Yazejian

TEACHERS COLLEGE PRESS
TEACHERS COLLEGE | COLUMBIA UNIVERSITY
NEW YORK AND LONDON

1-800-334-2014 · www.kaplanco.com

Published simultaneously by Teachers College Press, 1234 Amsterdam Avenue, New York, NY 10027 and Kaplan Early Learning Company, 1310 Lewisville-Clemmons Rd., Lewisville, NC 27023

Copyright © 2019 by Teachers College, Columbia University

Cover photo by Zero Creatives / Getty Images

All rights reserved. No part of this publication may be reproduced or transmitted in any form or by any means, electronic or mechanical, including photocopy, or any information storage and retrieval system, without permission from the publisher. For reprint permission and other subsidiary rights requests, please contact Teachers College Press, Rights Dept.: tcpressrights@tc.columbia.edu

Library of Congress Cataloging-in-Publication Data

Names: Seplocha, Holly, author.
Title: Coaching with ECERS : strategies and tools to improve quality in pre-K & K classrooms / Holly Seplocha ; foreword by Debby Cryer, Richard M. Clifford, Thelma Harms, and Noreen Yazejian.
Description: New York, NY : Teachers College Press, [2019] | Includes bibliographical references and index. |
Identifiers: LCCN 2018037455 (print) | LCCN 2018047110 (ebook) | ISBN 9780807777480 (ebook) | ISBN 9780807759547 (paper : acid-free paper)
Subjects: LCSH: Early childhood education—Evaluation. | Classroom environment—Evaluation. | Mentoring in education.
Classification: LCC LB1139.23 (ebook) | LCC LB1139.23 .S46 2019 (print) | DDC 372.21—dc23
LC record available at https://lccn.loc.gov/2018037455

ISBN 978-0-8077-5954-7 (paper)
ISBN 978-0-8077-7748-0 (ebook)

Printed on acid-free paper
Manufactured in the United States of America

26 25 24 23 22 21 20 19   8 7 6 5 4 3 2 1

Contents

PART II: COACHING WITH ECERS SUBSCALES

Foreword

Since the first edition of *Early Childhood Environment Rating Scale*, by Thelma Harms and Richard M. Clifford, was published in 1980, a primary focus of the scale has been to guide program improvement. As the story goes, early childhood practitioners asked the authors what they needed to do to provide high-quality care and education for young children in their programs, and the authors responded with a roadmap to quality, or the ECERS. Since then, new Environment Rating Scales have been developed to be used with groups of children in specific settings and with different ages, new authors have been added, and new editions created. But the goal of using the scales to measure and improve what children receive in early childhood settings has never changed.

The scales have a long history of being used to guide program improvement. People setting up programs have referred to them in designing facilities, equipping classrooms, and training teachers. The U.S. military began early systematic use of the scales across branches, with the Navy and Army using them in the early 1980s. Individual early childhood programs, local agencies, and some states followed closely with program improvement efforts guided by the ECERS. Use of the scales in program improvement efforts has spread throughout the world.

In the United States, the scales have now become heavily used in quality rating and improvement systems (QRIS). These systems, as well as requirements for program improvement in other large systems such as Head Start, have provided the field with a greatly increased number of professionals who, in cooperation with program staff, encourage the growth of quality in many early childhood settings. Referred to as coaches, technical assistance providers, mentors, master teachers, or other job titles, they all face enormous challenges in helping the staff of early childhood programs change what they do to encourage better child development and school readiness. This is an arduous task indeed, and there are few, if any, definitive resources that coaches can use to understand the complex skills and understandings required to make program improvement efforts successful. Very often it has been a "fly by the seat of your pants" kind of job, where the most guidance a new coach can expect is through friendly chats with more experienced peers. Over time, changes in program quality have certainly been evident as child-care and education programs have participated in program improvement efforts with coaches. But the job of coaching might have been less rocky if new coaches had been able to access a resource that provided the basics to doing the job.

The authors of the scales have created training materials on how to score and understand the ERS requirements. Other groups and individuals have also tried to create materials that help to improve programs through explaining what the scales' requirements mean. However, these are not materials a coach can pick up and say, "Oh! These are the issues I will have to deal with. This is what I am supposed to do!" This book is an answer to the lack of resources specially designed for program improvement professionals who work with the ECERS.

This book represents a well-considered view of the intricacies inherent in providing program improvement assistance through coaching, using either the ECERS-R or the ECERS-3. It has been created by a highly respected author with lots of successful experience in the program assessment and improvement field. It concentrates on how to encourage quality improvement by working primarily with teachers as the frontline individuals who can make change happen for children. It also notes the importance of working with administrators. It discusses the what, when, how, and why of creating change, including building a trusting relationship with program staff and understanding the cycle of giving information to encourage change and following up, as well as giving detailed information on the specifics of working with each subscale of the ECERS.

Both experienced and novice coaches will find this resource of great value. It will be a reminder and a source of new ideas for the experienced, while acting as a clear and realistic source of the basics of TA for the new coach. It provides the theory and the facts, both necessary for coaching. We, the authors of the ECERS, thank Holly for writing this much-needed resource, and hope that the book eases the challenges that coaches face every day.

—*Debby Cryer, Richard M. Clifford, Thelma Harms, and Noreen Yazejian*, Authors of the ERS

Acknowledgments

My sincere thanks to the many coaches, master teachers, program directors, supervisors, and classroom teachers who have worked with me over the years to raise the quality of classrooms and teaching practices for all young children. I continue to learn from and be inspired by you. I am especially indebted to Mary DeBlasio and Amy Gaul for our countless ongoing discussions and questions about understanding ECERS-R and ECERS-3 and what is good for preschool children. Special thanks to Renee Whelan for her gracious assistance and work on Chapter 1 and coaching teachers.

I am grateful to ERS authors Thelma Harms, Dick Clifford, Debby Cryer, and Noreen Yazejian for not only developing and revising the instrument but also for our many conversations and emails to help me understand and use the ECERS as intended. To Debby Cryer and Cathy Riley and the ERSI team, thank you for guiding me to be a highly reliable user of ECERS. I learn so much from our reliability observations and ongoing discussions. Thanks to Sarah Biondello, senior acquisitions editor at Teachers College Press, for your time, guidance, persistence, and especially your patience in working with me in this endeavor. Lastly, a special thank you to Maria Conforti for her gentle nudging ("Did you write today?") and friendship.

Introduction

Helping early childhood teachers and programs grow and improve has been my life's work since I left being a preschool and kindergarten teacher. I have worked as a classroom teacher as well as a mentor, coach, supervisor, program director, executive director, teacher educator, and researcher. Being able to know firsthand the postures and operations of varied positions and sectors affords me an advantage in bringing the perspectives of best practices in early childhood education to this book. My passion and the unifying focus for my work continue to be improving the quality of education for all young children.

Teaching young children is never easy, though it is infinitely rewarding. Being a teacher is energizing, draining, exciting, challenging, and never boring. It takes more than just enjoying being with young children. Being a preschool or kindergarten teacher requires:

- Patience
- Creativity
- Enthusiasm
- Flexibility
- Humor
- Dedication
- Respect for diversity
- Knowledge of and appreciation for the development and learning of young children
- Support and appreciation for the uniqueness of families

In this era of assessment to ensure high quality, being a preschool or kindergarten teacher also takes knowing and using the Early Childhood Environment Rating Scales (both ECERS-3 and ECERS-R).

Being a coach, mentor, supervisor, or administrator who works with preschool and/or kindergarten teachers requires that you know and understand how young children learn, and developmentally appropriate practices (DAPs) that support growth and development. It also requires that you have skills in observation, giving feedback, adult learning, and understanding how to make classroom improvements that last. And, yes, it also takes knowing and using the Early Childhood Environment Rating Scales (ECERS-3 and ECERS-R).

DESIGN OF THE BOOK

This book provides a framework for using ECERS as a coaching tool to impact quality in preschool and kindergarten classrooms. Although ECERS is used to assess the overall quality of preschool and kindergarten classrooms, this is not about teaching to the tool. Instead, we examine ECERS subscales with an eye on the benefits to children by using best practices. Strategies and tools for coaches to use in their work with teachers and/or administrators are presented. By improving classrooms and teaching practices, scores will rise, not just for the day, but ideally for every day.

Part I, "All About Coaching," provides the context for coaching teachers and/or the program director in a way that has meaning and impacts classroom practice.

Chapter 1, "Basic Tenets of Coaching," reviews how adults learn and sets the stage for working with teachers of 3- to 5-year-olds. Since open dialogue and communication are the foundation for coaching, it focuses on the importance of building a relationship with the teacher and administrator.

Chapter 2, "Many Hats of Coaches," examines the diverse roles of those who coach early childhood teachers, from peer coaching, to coaching from the inside or outside of the program, to administrators and supervisors who coach within their role. The nuances of coaching teachers based on where they are in their teaching experience and knowledge are discussed. It also presents the case for building on-site program capacity for QRIS coaches who target their efforts with administrators to coach with ECERS.

Chapter 3, "Coaching Using ECERS," provides a rationale for using ECERS-3 or ECERS-R as a vehicle to improve classrooms for children. Contrary to the idea of simply getting a good score on the day the instrument is administered, the purpose of ECERS is to impact outcomes for children. Strategies and tools for giving feedback and using a strengths-based approach to coaching are included.

Part II, "Coaching with ECERS Subscales," is the heart of this book. Chapter 4 provides a context for using the subscales and an overview of the differences between ECERS-3 and ECERS-R. The remaining six chapters in this part each address an individual subscale. All chapters follow the same format, beginning with the benefits to children for the particular subscale and then presenting suggestions for quick and easy fixes and strategies for classroom change that generally take more time for teachers to understand and incorporate the change into daily practice. These are followed with recommendations for fine-tuning good quality into higher quality. Each chapter concludes with ideas that coaches can use for group meetings, professional learning communities, or staff workshops.

Part III, "Putting It All Together," merges strategies for coaching and addressing ECERS Items. In Chapter 11 I discuss coaching through group meetings and professional development activities, and partnerships between coaches and administrators. Also included are overall ECERS Tips to impact quality. Chapter 12 offers final thoughts, bringing the reader back to the why of ECERS and the purpose of coaching with ECERS (Improving Quality for Children). In addition, we incorporate how and why to avoid pussyfooting around issues. The section "No, No, Never, Nevers" outlines practices that exemplify poor, uniformed practice, which then result in lower scores. The book concludes with resources for coaches and teachers, including Internet resources, articles, webinars, and videos to use in coaching and learning more about best practice, as well as ECERS.

As you use this book, whether you are a coach, an administrator, or a classroom teacher, I encourage you to continue to find wonder and new challenges and opportunities in all that you do to support the growth and learning of young children and their teachers. ECERS isn't about getting a good score; it's about doing what's best for children.

ALL ABOUT COACHING

CHAPTER 1

Basic Tenets of Coaching

Coaching may be one of the most powerful ways to improve the quality of preschool classrooms to ensure positive outcomes for children. In its simplest form, coaching is helping a teacher to develop and grow. Although there are varied strategies for coaching—from modeling a strategy, to giving advice, to observing and giving feedback—coaching teachers is about enhancing existing knowledge, developing or refining skills and strategies, and fostering reflection. A coach is an advocate for best practice. The central purpose of coaching is to promote the development and growth of young children through empowering and supporting the adults who work with them.

Ideally, coaches, teachers, and administrators form a program improvement team to discuss classroom strengths and address needed improvements. Directors are often called the "gatekeepers to quality." As administrators oversee budgets, order supplies, arrange for maintenance and repairs, establish policies and procedures, and foster the vision and culture of the program, their involvement in program improvement is important. Although many Items can be improved through effective coaching of teachers, some Items are out of the teachers' control. If a program improvement team is not feasible, minimally, the coach should keep the administrator aware of classroom improvements and bring forward those Items that need administrative support in order to improve.

Quality involves choice. Although no classroom or program scores a "7" on all ECERS Items, directors/principals need to choose Items in the administrative domain that they can realistically support and those Items that are too costly or impractical to fix. For example, although a teacher can improve how she supervises children on the playground, and how she interacts to support their development and learning, the teacher cannot install fencing around the playground or change the playground surface. The administrator can, however, have repairs made to fencing and gates to make the playground safer.

As an advocate for best practice, the coach works with teachers (or coaches directors in the coaching of teachers) on observable teaching behaviors, practices, room arrangement, and so forth, that are within the scope of the teachers' role. The coach also works with administrators to inform them of Items that need their support, and can help the administrator to examine the feasibility and practicality of making structural improvements and equipment and material purchases.

ADULT LEARNING

We know that for young children, learning is an active process, as children learn through their experiences and interactions with people, places, and things. The same holds true for adults. Learning is an active process for teachers. Teachers make meaning through their prior knowledge and experiences and current roles. Teachers learn each and every day in the classroom as they plan and implement lessons and environments, actively engage in professional development, and interact with other teachers, administrators, and coaches.

Learning is, however, the ultimate responsibility of the learner. Teacher coaches can't *make* a teacher change any more than a soccer coach can *make* a goalie prevent each shot on goal from going into the net. The role of the coach is to facilitate growth. It is helping teachers to learn rather than teaching them how to teach. Although there are certainly effective and ineffective strategies for teaching young children, there is no magic "one right way" to teach. Teachers learn to be better teachers with coaching that unlocks their potential to understand and use best practice.

Ideas influence action. As teachers learn effective ingredients and parameters for preschool classroom environments and new strategies for supporting children's growth, learners construct their own knowledge. ECERS provides guidance in best practice, and these ideas can help to frame the action needed. For example, the concept of interest centers versus play areas is an idea new to many teachers. Understanding how interest centers impact children's learning is vital for teachers to grasp in order to take the needed action to arrange and equip learning centers to maximize child outcomes. Without understanding the reasons for ECERS Items and how change can impact classroom quality for children, any change made is at best short-lived and not thoroughly incorporated into daily practice.

ADULT LEARNERS

Adults have life experiences that shape and color their perspectives and attitudes. The experience and knowledge base of the adult learner is an "important resource for learning . . . adults can call upon their past experiences and prior knowledge in formulating learning" (Caffarella & Barnett, 1994, p. 30). Current teachers have had many teachers of their own throughout their prior schooling. The best teachers are often remembered as caring, nurturing individuals who made learning fun and encouraged thinking among the learners in their class. They are also remembered because they treated their students as individuals, listened to them, and provided help when needed. A coach can help teachers to build on these past experiences and knowledge by encouraging teachers to reflect on their favorite teachers (at any grade level) and what skills and dispositions she had that caused him to be effective. Reflecting on prior negative experiences with teachers to identify what was *wrong* with a teacher, or an experience, is an important part of the exercise as well.

Adults have a great many preoccupations inside and outside the confines of their jobs or particular learning situation. Like all adults, for preschool teachers to find a balance between work and life is often difficult. Many have children of their own, are dealing with aging parents, have outside responsibilities, are involved in their communities, have partners and relationship needs, and lead busy and frenetic lives. Often underpaid in comparison to their public school counterparts, preschool teachers may also lack societal status and respect. Coaches need to consider these preoccupations as they work with teachers to ensure they are being realistic regarding time frames and support needed. As adults, teachers have real decisions to make and real problems both in and out of the classroom.

Change is not easy. For most people, doing what they've always done or are doing now is comfortable. It's like putting on a pair of old shoes. You may know that the shoes are worn out or even have leaks when worn in wet weather, but new shoes means shopping, expense, and then breaking them in to your feet and style. In addition, there are all those newer shoes in your closet that you wore once or only a few times, so why buy another new pair? Many teachers attend workshops on required topics or those of interest; they walk away with handouts or notes that often simply get filed or lost or tossed out. Sometimes teachers take away one new idea or activity to try that may or may not get implemented without support or follow-up. Change is not something most adults seek. It can be time-consuming, fraught with problems, and somewhat painful and fear inducing.

ADULTS IN PRESCHOOL AND KINDERGARTEN

As anyone who has ever taught preschool or kindergarten will tell you, teaching young children is not easy. To be an effective early childhood teacher means having knowledge and understanding of how young children learn and grow, developmentally appropriate practice (DAP), and effective learning environments. It is also equally important to know how to observe and listen to children to develop curriculum that follows children's interests and how to purposefully interact with children to support their learning.

Teachers come to the classroom with varied educational backgrounds and prior experiences with children and education. They also come with varied dispositions and internally held beliefs and values about children, parenting, and teaching. These experiences and beliefs have obvious impact on their practice.

For example, a teacher may *believe* that children learn best when the teacher is in front of the class *teaching*. In that classroom, children spend a large portion of the day in whole group doing the same thing, often responding to rote and repetition. Free play is seen as a time for the children to *play* while the teacher catches up on paperwork, handles discipline, and prepares for the next lessons.

Another teacher may *believe* that children learn best through active exploration with teachers who scaffold children's learning through listening, observing, asking questions, and interacting. In this classroom, whole-group time is short and purposeful in building community and introducing ideas and concepts. Free play is valued as an important time for learning, and the teacher's role is to trust children, follow their interests, and engage with individuals to follow the child's lead to support learning and differentiate interactions.

All teachers want their children to learn and to behave. The coach's role is to capitalize on this common goal. No one wants to be a bad teacher. Teachers don't walk into a classroom saying to themselves, "I want to be the worst teacher. How can I mess up my children today?" All teachers have good intentions, but not all practice is effective. ECERS provides an objective vehicle for research-based best practice.

In addition, with the growing focus in our country on accountability and outcomes, preschool and kindergarten teachers feel the weight of administration, families, and public opinion. Teachers may feel that, to show student achievement, they cannot teach in child-centered and developmentally appropriate ways; rather, they may feel that they must fill children with as much information as possible so each child is *ready* for the next grade. Although it's true that preschool and kindergarten can provide the foundational support for later academic success, this is only true if programs are high quality (Barnett, 2011; Camilli, Vargas, Ryan, & Barnett, 2010; Colker & Koralek, 2018). In other words, simply attending preschool, while there may be short-term gains, isn't what matters. It is the quality of the classroom that supports future outcomes. ECERS is the most widely used tool to measure the overall global quality of preschool programs and individual kindergarten classrooms to benefit children.

BUILDING A RELATIONSHIP

There are many factors that go into building a strong and beneficial relationship between coaches and teachers. For instance:

- Trust
- Listening
- Degree of formality

- Time and pacing
- Reflective cycle

We will now go into each of these factors in detail.

Trust

Trust is the foundation to building positive working relationships. As we know, there are many articles and books that have been written—for educational organizations, businesses, leadership, and so forth—with trust being one of the most critical elements for success. The coach has to establish trusting relationships with his teachers for this collaborative reflective process to occur and to truly refine teaching practices.

Ways to establish trusting relationships between and among coaches, teachers, and administrators include establishing upfront the importance of being open and honest in their work with each other, shared expectations, reliability, and meaning what you say. Children need professional adults to care for them, who model trusting relationships, and who do not create or tolerate toxic environments.

One of the biggest deterrents to trust encountered by coaches is teachers' impressions that the coach is feeding the administrator information that will negatively impact the teachers, especially in relation to their evaluations. Although it is important for the coach to work in partnership with administrators, some teachers may be hesitant to share their problems in the classroom or lack of understanding in a particular area if they feel this information may influence their internal annual evaluation. The coach shares with administrators general trends in classrooms and focus areas based on the data the coach collects. If a sensitive issue has arisen, the coach should ask the teacher's permission to share with the administrator or she may guide the teacher in sharing the information. If children's safety is in jeopardy or the teacher is exhibiting harmful practices, the coach must tell the teacher that he needs to inform the administration for assistance to resolve the matter. In addition, the coach cannot tell other teachers about her colleague's needs unless a teacher is seeking help from peers. Peer-to-peer support can be the most influential change agent; however, when encouraged, there needs to be willingness to learn from another teacher with a defined purpose in mind.

This is not to imply that coaches shouldn't have open discussions with the program administrators. The evidence for a relationship between effective leadership and program quality is growing. Indeed, many outside coaches who support their state or county's QRIS also coach administrators in coaching their teachers. Coaches whose role it is to coach teachers also need to develop a strong, trusting relationship with the program administrator. Whenever possible, the administrator should be part of the improvement team. Because some ECERS Items are out of the teacher's control, teaming with the administrator enables the administrator to take responsibility for making improvements possible.

Listening

Listening is a skill that is not always easy to do in our fast-paced world where we each have lots to accomplish as well as many time constraints. However, if we do not listen to one another, there is no point in continuing the conversation. Listening is a component of understanding and respecting the other person in a relationship. It is a skill that coaches must practice with teachers in order to help teachers succeed to help their children to succeed.

When you are in a coaching situation, are you just waiting to talk? When coaching, there is a tendency to do all the talking because one wants to provide feedback to help the teacher. Actually, the opposite approach is best. A coach should lead with questions to determine background knowledge, help teacher reflection, and support the recognition of what needs to be done next in the classroom to improve quality. Do you listen more than you talk? When coaching, you may have teachers who want you to provide them with all the information. However, one must still stop to question the teacher and to ask for his input, to reiterate what he took from the conversation. To do this well requires a coach to be a good listener.

Degree of Formality

As coaches and teachers establish relationships with each other, there may be moments where the coach feels like a psychologist because teachers may share personal issues that are affecting their instructional practices. Coaches must be mindful of their role at all times. They are mentors; they are not trying to be someone's friend or supervisor. A coach must not convey that there are favorite teachers in the school. If a coach does show favoritism, the integrity of supporting all assigned teachers becomes possibly tangled with a culture of competition, resentment, or disinterest.

Time and Pacing

In order to create a good working relationship with those in the setting, it is crucial for coaches to set a systematic approach to their visits. Coaches need to be able to contribute to the reflective cycle with the teacher and/or administrator. However, you cannot arbitrarily set a number of classroom visits that should occur each day or how much time should be spent in each classroom. Each teacher is different, and as we encourage differentiating our instruction for children, the same applies with teachers.

Here are some time management tips that have worked for coaches:

1. Set up a calendar that is visible and user-friendly where modifications can be easily made.
2. After meeting with each teacher in the beginning of the year, let them know that you will be scheduling meetings to discuss focus areas and the structured observation tool criteria, ECERS.
3. Schedule the collaboratively determined day or approximate day that you will be visiting the classroom.
4. Then schedule a post-visit conference within a few days after the classroom visit.

There will also be times when you will simply check in with teachers by stopping in for a few minutes, possibly conducting an on-the-spot demonstration; or having a quick conversation; or sharing a few tips as well as supporting or facilitating a professional learning community (PLC). Time management is key to visibility. Since visiting classrooms is the priority, manage your time between the new teachers who may need the most support and the veterans who may be looking for a challenge. Differentiating and managing your time is key to your success.

Reflective Cycle

The reflective cycle is at the heart of coaching practices. Coaches using the reflective cycle go through a cyclical reflective process to improve instructional practices (see Figure 1.1).

This process is similar to clinical supervision, which involves observing and reviewing teaching practice for the purpose of improvement and usually

Figure 1.1. Coaching with a Reflective Cycle

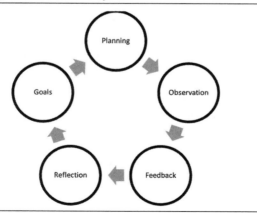

includes evaluation; however, in coaching, the reflective cycle process is not evaluative since the coach is not a supervisor. The process is also similar to the cognitive coaching model, which involves the teacher exploring her thinking behind her action or practice with the coach facilitating through asking questions (e.g., what was your goal when you paused to interact in the dramatic play center?). When using the ECERS to support quality in early childhood education, the following scenario provides a simple example of the reflective cycle at its finest.

After a PLC where a veteran teacher and coach co-facilitate a review of the ECERS criteria as well as the purpose in using the instrument, teachers conduct a self-assessment that is given to the coach for his review. The coach schedules the pre-visit conference to discuss the self-assessment and asks the teacher if she has any questions or needs clarification and/or support. During this pre-visit conference, a discussion of the teacher's goals should be at the forefront (possibly with the previous year's recommendations and focus areas at the table). The coach is prepared with the instrument and data to inform the discussion. The teacher explains to the coach her next steps, and collaboratively they decide when the coach will visit the classroom to administer the ECERS. The coach lets the teacher know that he is available to answer any other questions that may come up later and provides the teacher with a couple of resources to further explain the criteria.

The coach keeps to his schedule and comes in on time prepared with the instrument and any other necessary materials. The coach models respect and reliable administration of the instrument by following all the ECERS guidelines. For example, the coach does not engage in conversations with the teacher during the observation and stays for the entire recommended time inclusive of going outside with the class and checking bathroom procedures.

After the ECERS observation, the coach reflects on the visit and uses the notes to score the Items. The coach prepares for the post-visit conference by generating recommendations that will be discussed during this feedback session.

The teacher and coach meet within a couple of days of the ECERS observation visit to reflect on practices, refer to the criteria in the instrument, and determine next steps. The goals are collaboratively decided on during this post-visit conference. Again, the coach leads with questions to determine which areas may need further clarification. The coach keeps the conversation objective by referring to the criteria and does not state an opinion during the discussion. The recommended feedback that was previously determined may be added to or slightly revised based on this reflective conversation. The goals always have children's safety as the top priority and should be specific, measurable, achievable and agreed upon, realistic, and timely (SMART goal). Goals should also be on improvements that are within the teacher's control (e.g., interactions, room arrangement, and discipline). Items beyond the teacher's control (e.g., facility, needed materials, and meal components) should be discussed with the administrator. The coach and teacher end with setting a time for a follow-up visit within several weeks to determine if next steps have been achieved. The reflective cycle continues on.

REFLECTION

Coaching focuses on the adult as a learner. Coaches recognize that the adults they coach have varied prior experiences, education, and beliefs about how children learn. Adults also have a great many distractions, both personal and professional, that impact their interests and needs as well as their dispositions for growth and change. At the heart of coaching is the relationship between the coach and the adult. Whether one is coaching teachers or coaching directors to coach teachers, building an open, trusting relationship is paramount to effective coaching. Effective coaches help adults grow by asking questions, encouraging reflection, building on strengths, and providing resources and feedback. ECERS provides an objective assessment of overall classroom quality and serves as a vehicle to identify strengths and areas needing improvement.

CHAPTER 2

Many Hats of Coaches

The first step in coaching in order to effect change is to develop relationships. Relationships are central to coaching and impact its effectiveness. Relationships lead to trust, and trust leads to receptivity and responsiveness (Curtis, Lebo, Cividanes, & Carter, 2013). Coaches come in many different forms and capacities. Because coaches come from varied internal and external positions, and may or may not have an existing relationship with the teacher, it is important to understand the nuances of coaching from varied roles.

Coaches may be any of the following:

- Someone the teacher already has a relationship with in a noncoaching capacity, such as a supervisor, director, administrator, or peer.
- Someone internal to the organization for whom coaching is part of her job, such as a master teacher, head teacher, or education coordinator. In this case the coach already has a relationship with the teacher.
- Someone external to the school or center, such as a QRIS coach or a consultant. In this case the coach will have limited to no prior relationship with the teacher.

ROLE CLARITY

What is your role? What are your intentions? In our experiences, if a teacher or administrator is unaware of a coach's role—regardless of a genuine attempt to improve children's learning and experiences in a collaborative manner—the coach's impact only scrapes the surface rather than deepens the teacher's knowledge and influence in the classroom.

The coach is similar to a mentor. He is a resource, someone who guides and supports teaching practices through a collaborative and reflective approach. The focus is on children's learning and how the teacher's instructional practices influence that learning. The coach is open, honest, and wants to learn from the teacher, too. One is constantly trying to learn more effective ways to support teachers and is considered a researcher as well as a practitioner. In the capacity of a researcher, the coach grounds decisions on scientifically based evidence.

The coach needs to explain the nature of her work to the teacher. In some schools and state QRIS systems, the nature of the coaches' work is well established. For example, in New Jersey, the coach's role has been clearly defined for public school districts' preschool programs in regulations and the preschool guidelines. Some effective coaches deliver a presentation to all the teachers at the beginning of the school year explaining their role, with opportunities for teachers to ask questions to clarify their understanding of the role. Additionally, coaches set up meetings with each of their assigned teachers from the start to review their role as well as begin the reflective cycle process, which begins with an area of focus that is associated with ECERS and goals.

If everyone has a clear understanding of the coach's role from the onset of support (especially when as a coach, you are also their director, principal, or supervisor), there will be less confusion and more buy-in to learn together. The coach's role will need clarity along the journey, which is the process of building an open and positive working relationship. As the relationship evolves, the level of support evolves.

QRIS TEAM SUPPORTING THE DIRECTOR AS COACH

Because leadership is a critical factor in quality early childhood programs, many state and county QRISs are moving away from providing coaches to coach teachers and moving toward coaches to coach the director. These QRIS coaches coach the director to coach teachers and to establish appropriate procedures and foundations for continuous quality improvement. In addition, with the high rate of staff turnover in many child-care programs (Whitebook, McClean, & Austin, 2016), it makes practical and fiscal sense to coach directors who tend to be more stable and can in turn coach new teachers when they join the program.

The director/administrator of an ECE program wears many hats. In a typical week, the director may fulfill the roles of counselor, cook, teacher, receptionist, plumber, fiscal expert, beggar, consoler, motivator, trainer, role model, disciplinarian, computer expert, magician, public speaker, child advocate, handyperson, and wizard of everything. The job is both complex and central to the operation of the program. With all these competing demands for a director's time, effective leadership is necessary to improve ECE programs and to maintain quality. In addition, many early childhood directors rise through the ranks of the field with little specialized training in management or leadership. On the other hand, some directors may have greater knowledge in business practices and organizational skills than they have in developmentally appropriate preschool teaching and learning. The sink-or-swim method of induction into the administrative role seems to prevail.

Coaching directors can impact quality by developing the skills of the director to balance and support organizational and fiscal skills, and early childhood programming.

The director manages internal functions that are likely to affect program quality. These may include, but are not limited to, recruiting, selecting and orienting staff; managing finances; negotiating conflict; creating the climate for a healthy organization; providing technical support and innovation; and leading a commitment to vision and mission. External functions may include garnering resources and allocating them wisely; collaborating widely; supporting and involving families; advocating for public policy; buffering staff; building coalitions of support; managing public relations; ensuring full enrollments; and leading a commitment to vision and mission. A QRIS coach, therefore, often serves as a resource person to the director to provide guidance, strategies, and information to support the director's organizational needs.

Administrators also play a vital role in creating a positive atmosphere through their beliefs, attitudes, expectations, and activities. Effective directors must be able to create a strong sense of community that includes shared values, common goals, and high expectations for both children's growth and learning, and staff performance. One of the coach's roles is in helping the director to articulate a vision grounded in developmentally appropriate practice. If a director or principal expects teachers to use workbooks and rote teaching, this has obvious negative impact on classroom practice and ECERS scores.

ECERS provides an objective, research-based framework for best practices for children. Effective QRIS coaches, therefore, focus improvement efforts beyond paperwork, policies, and procedures to impact classroom quality that benefits children. Discussion of ECERS Items and Indicators is vital. This often forms the foundation for the QRIS coach's work with the director by ensuring that the director is not only knowledgeable in the scale but also understands the benefits to children.

Directors have clear and direct impact on classroom quality as evidenced by ECERS Items in a variety of ways. They are generally responsible for:

- Space and ensuring maintenance.
- Access to gross motor space and equipment including fencing, bollards, safety surface, and safety of the playground equipment.
- Purchasing appropriate classroom materials.
- Classroom schedules.
- Purchasing supplies to support health and sanitation procedures.
- Classroom observations *and* feedback to staff.

Coaching to improve classroom practice begins with collating ECERS scores by Item and subscale across the program. This process identifies both areas of strength and areas needing improvement. The coach celebrates the strengths of the program by making sure teachers are aware of the common areas of high quality. The coach and director then examine the common areas needing improvement. Looking at the areas can inform topics for professional development and/or staff meetings, additional materials needed, and areas on which to focus coaching efforts, as well as areas that are not feasible or too costly to address.

The director and coach can develop a plan of action, including time frames, resources needed, and tasks to be completed. The director then implements the plan, targeting three to five Items at a time. The coach continues to serve as a resource to the director, which may involve modeling a coaching feedback session with a teacher and/or assisting the director in planning a workshop or staff meeting activities. As the QRIS coach works with multiple programs, his time onsite is limited. Often coaching is more intensive at the beginning of the relationship to help to develop the plan, and then maintaining communication and support as the capacity of the director grows and the plan progresses. As one NJ QRIS coach remarked, "My role is to coach myself out of a job."

Meaningful growth and change are accomplished through an understanding that the people who work at a school must be empowered in their efforts to grow professionally. The QRIS coach is a catalyst in identifying problem areas and helping administrators to analyze the situation to find workable solutions. Decisions made by the director commit the program to a given course of action and a level of quality.

COACHES COME IN MANY ROLES

The job titles of coaches are many and varied, and often the individual has other job responsibilities beyond coaching teachers. Whether the coach comes from inside or outside the organization, there are nuances to coaching from varied roles.

Director/Principal as Coach

The key issue for those in this role is that you are also the teacher's boss and/ or evaluator. Although this affords a present relationship and assumes a degree of trust, the relationship is hierarchical and the trust is framed by the existing role. As an administrator, central to coaching to effect change is to differentiate between supervision and evaluation versus coaching. The teacher needs to know that your coaching relationship is separate and needs to trust that it will not impact evaluations. This is accomplished through both explicit word as well as deed. I recommend a frank conversation to discuss, listen, and explore feelings. The purpose of coaching is to improve classrooms for children.

Shared vision for children should be the common ground. Teachers should know when an observation is for coaching purposes and participate in establishing the ECERS focus for the coaching cycle. ECERS observations should not be vehicles for "snoopervision." Teachers should also know when an observation is for evaluation purposes and be aware of the evaluation form/tool being used. It is not recommended that an ECERS score be used for staff evaluation. Establishing clarity and distinction between supervision and coaching should not be neglected.

Master Teacher/Head Teacher/Education Coordinator as Coach

A person in this role often has the advantage of already knowing the teacher as they work in the same building or program. The disadvantage is that of being in the middle between classroom teachers and administrators. Confidentiality is therefore central for effective coaching. The teacher needs to know and trust that what she says and does during the coaching sessions, unless harmful to children or illegal, will not be shared with administration or other staff. Coaching is about growing teachers in the best interest of children.

QRIS Support Team as Coach

In this role, you gain both an inside and outside perspective. Generally, there is no existing relationship, and often the teacher or administrator is unaware of what your role as a coach is. Sharing a little about yourself and your experiences as well as learning about the teacher and administrator forms the foundation for a relationship. Discussing your role and its parameters including how often you will be on-site, and establishing a framework for coaching observations and visits provides clarity to the teacher and program at the beginning of the relationship.

It is easy in this role to get caught up in simply improving ECERS scores. Although this is a natural outcome of effective coaching, it is important to always bring the purpose back to best practices for children. This creates more lasting change as the teacher begins to internalize the *why* of what needs to be changed or fine-tuned, not just *what* she needs to be doing when being observed for her school's quality rating. As this is sometimes a short-lived assignment (as a preparation for ratings), be careful not to overwhelm the teacher with too much at one time. It is recommended that you coach based on no more than one subscale at a time.

Consultant as Coach

Consultants are in many ways similar to QRIS support teams in that they share an outside perspective and have been brought in by the school or program to support the teaching staff's understanding and implementation of ECERS global process quality. Consultants need a deep understanding of ECERS as well as the benefits of high-quality practice for children. Coaching may involve group workshops, observations of classrooms using ECERS, and individual mentoring. The key difference between QRIS support teams and consultants is that consultants are being paid by the program and they report to the director or administrator. Role clarity is particularly important in this case as is an open, well-defined framework. For trust to be developed, teachers need to have confidence that the consultant is working with them in the best interests of children.

Peer as Coach

Peer coaching is usually an informal relationship between teachers to support each other in their implementation of ECERS requirements in their classrooms and practice. Peer coaches have a deep inside perspective as both coach and teacher work in the same school in the same capacity and using the same curriculum and procedures. Coaching involves observing each other's classrooms and sharing ideas and tips about teaching and children. It also entails developing a shared understanding of the nuances of ECERS.

USING DEVELOPMENTALLY APPROPRIATE PRACTICES IN COACHING

The parameters of developmentally appropriate practice (DAP) (Copple, Bredekamp, Koralek, & Charner, 2013) for children also apply in working with teachers. To be developmentally appropriate for children means teachers respond to where children are in terms of their development, culture, interests, and prior experiences. To be developmentally appropriate in coaching adults means that coaches respond to teachers where they are. The Center for the Study of Child Care Employment (Whitebook, McClean, & Austin, 2016) notes that the overwhelming majority of the child-care and education workforce is women. Other statistics reported that the average age of the teachers is 39 and 35% have at least a bachelor's degree. In applying DAP to coaching teachers, you need to consider:

- Adult development and learning that is age and stage appropriate. Activities, materials, interactions, and experiences need to be safe, healthy, interesting, achievable, and challenging to support teachers where they are in their lives and teaching experiences.
- Strengths, interests, and needs of the individual teacher. Coaching needs to be strength-based and a partnership between coach and teacher to address areas of need based on the teacher's interest, concerns, knowledge, and assets.

- Knowledge of the social and cultural contexts in which teachers live to ensure that coaching is meaningful, relevant, and respectful.

Like children, different teachers are not the same, not on the same skill level, and come to the classroom with varied experiences and knowledge. Effective coaches see the strengths and successes of individuals they coach and help them perform even better. Using DAP in coaching means accepting the teachers where they are and guiding them to learn and grow.

Stages of Teachers

Similar to stages of development of children, teachers also progress through stages in teacher development. Lillian Katz's seminal work (1972) on stages of teachers identified four stages through which teachers progress as they gain experience: survival, consolidations, renewal, and maturity. Here, we apply these stages to the coaching needs of teachers.

- *Survival:* New teachers with 0 to 2 years of experience. Their goals are getting through the day, no one getting hurt, and not losing any children. For many, classroom management and discipline are of primary concern. Although they may have learned what good practice is, and even seen it in action, they often rationalize that it won't work with these children in their classroom and they often revert to reliance on a teacher-directed style. They question whether teaching is really for them, and if they can in fact teach. Coaching teachers in survival mode needs to be very focused and specific, selecting those ECERS Items initially that will have the greatest impact on reducing any chaos, ensuring safety and healthy environments, adjusting daily schedules and room arrangements, and positive approaches to classroom management. Specific guidance in ECERS-3 Items 3, 8–11, 32, and 33 (ECERS-R Items 4, 10–14, 31, and 34) is the place to begin. Although it is always important to focus on the benefits to children, teachers in this stage may need to simply be given materials and resources, as well as shown what to do specifically to survive the day. It is important that their specific needs are addressed and multiple suggestions and options for handling concerns be given and discussed.
- *Consolidation:* Generally, teachers in their second year of teaching through year 3, and sometimes year 4, are in this stage. They have survived and are beginning to learn what works and what doesn't. They have begun to focus on the needs of individual children and instruction. Although they may have a stronger handle on lesson planning and classroom management, the concerns of these teachers focus around managing certain children, for instance:

a particularly disruptive child; or a child whose language they don't speak; or a child who seems to be progressing slower than others. Coaching teachers in this stage means discussions about what works and why, providing resources to address specific concerns, guiding to professional development, and support of networking with other teachers in this stage. Sharing ideas and strategies is key. Specific guidance in ECERS-3 subscales for Language and Literacy, Learning Activities, and Interaction (ECERS-R subscales Language-Reasoning, Activities, Interaction, and Item 37) based on observations and needs is most relevant.

- *Renewal:* Teachers generally enter this stage in their fourth year of teaching (though some sooner and some later). Teachers in this stage have confidence in their teaching and are interested in new ideas, lessons, strategies, and fine-tuning. They want to refresh and improve and add new twists to their teaching. They are often self-motivating. Coaching teachers in this stage means providing opportunities to grow and share with other teachers, sharing articles with new ideas and resources, and following their agenda of areas of interest and growth. The basics are there and good practice is evident. Based on their needs and observations, specific guidance to support ECERS-3 math, science, gross motor, and literacy Items (ECERS-R Items 17, 26, 28, 29, 32, and 38) is suggested.

- *Maturity:* Teachers generally enter this stage of their career after 5 or more years of teaching. They are still interested in new ideas and strategies but are also interested in purpose, research, philosophy, and reflection. They are comfortable and confident in their teaching but may also have picked up some bad habits along the way. Coaching teachers in this stage is most effective through discussion of the benefits to children and the why for any changes needed. Effective teachers in this stage benefit by sharing their expertise with others. Any ECERS-3 or ECERS-R Items based on observation and teachers' interests are appropriate to address.

Teachers go through these stages at their own pace, similar to children. It is also likely that they will fluctuate between stages based on personal life issues (e.g., caring for a parent or going through a divorce may move a teacher back into an earlier stage) or professional experience (e.g., changing to a new school or grade level or curriculum may move a teacher back to an earlier stage). A teacher may also get stuck in a stage due to being tired, burned out, or under excessive pressure. Through getting to know the teachers that one is coaching, listening to their concerns, questions, and issues, coaches can identify where the teacher is in her development and provide targeted support. By limiting ECERS coaching to specific subscales and/or Items, and targeting a specific focus, coaches increase the likelihood of success and facilitate quicker progress. As goals are achieved, it also creates confidence that additional goals can be achieved as well.

REFLECTION

Coaches come in many different roles from both inside and outside the organization that affect the relationship as well as how coaching occurs. These roles impact the framework for coaching. To develop and sustain a coaching relationship, attention must be given to clarifying the role of the coach. This helps to shed light on expectations of the coaching relationship and focus, and builds trust.

Coaches must also tune into the nuances of the stage of the teacher. Whether an outside coach working with teachers or a director who is coaching teachers, tailoring coaching to the needs based on stage supports the likelihood of impacting change. The stages presented for teachers are also applicable to directors who move from survival to maturity in similar ways. For coaches who coach administrators in program improvement, addressing the needs based on stage is equally important. Because the administrator has significant effect on the quality of the program, involving the director in the change process can ensure improvements are lasting.

CHAPTER 3

Coaching Using ECERS

Teachers who are given the opportunity to be co-constructors of knowledge feel valued, and their takeaway messages are more relevant and powerful. Developing classroom environments that empower students by respecting their ideas and contributions is foundational to ECERS. Effectively engaging teachers involves intentionally including the teacher in the changes, plans, and practices that promote children's learning.

QUALITY FOR CHILDREN IS THE COMMON GROUND

The environment of a classroom is one of the most powerful teaching tools available to preschool and kindergarten teachers.

Effective teachers promote teaching and learning that recognizes the strengths and abilities of students and cultivates the skills they need. Developmentally appropriate, foundational learning is critical for children's future success in school and life. Erika Christakis wrote in *The Importance of Being Little*: "Child centered doesn't mean child run, and warm and responsive early childhood settings are not the opposite of intellectually oriented ones" (2016, p. 74). Throughout the scales, ECERS-3 and ECERS-R support warm, caring, child-centered classrooms that also support child learning through appropriate materials, schedules and routines, learning activities, and engaging and purposeful interactions. ECERS embraces environments that provide for interactions and exploration through responsive intentional teaching.

Although one may differ in thoughts on the best curriculum to use, ECERS is curriculum blind and doesn't advocate one curriculum over another. ECERS presents—based on extensive research and validity—an instrument that illustrates the plethora of important aspects that go into effectively teaching young children. It is an objective view of many of the components necessary for high-quality classrooms that produce positive growth for young children. Although some teachers and programs consider ECERS as a vehicle to stage a classroom for the day of observation, in order for change to be lasting and beneficial to young children, a classroom needs to adhere to ECERS requirements each and every day. By comparing the scale requirements with the observed practice, coaches are able to work with teachers to make specific plans for changes that will work in the particular setting.

All teachers and programs want the best for young children. ECERS provides a tool to focus coaching through use of the subscales and Indicators as an objective standard to be explored and implemented. It is about reflecting about teaching and deepening our understanding and practice. A coach and teacher must always consider how specific ECERS observational notes link to effective practice. In other words, when we see children engaged as a teacher reads a story, what are they learning? When we see children acting out or not listening during a whole group story, what are they learning? When we see a teacher repeatedly interrupting a story to call attention to those who are not involved, children learn that to get the teacher's attention, you misbehave. For some children, any attention is better than none.

The common ground for coaching teachers is using specific, documented observations and quotes as a vehicle for discussion about what children learn from that specific experience or interaction. Coaches sometimes make the mistake of going into a diagnostic mode and prescribing a litany of fixes needed. In doing so, they rush into a fix that lacks the conceptual understanding needed for lasting change. Using ECERS to prioritize goals with the teacher, always bringing discussion back to the shared goal of what's best for children, helps to frame and give meaning to the "why" of the change. By focusing on the shared goal of what's best for children, coaches can work toward effecting change since the goal is ultimately not about what teachers do, but about the child's experiences. This takes the focus away from what the teacher is doing *wrong* to what children need in order to thrive in the classroom.

GIVING FEEDBACK TO SUPPORT GROWTH

Coaching teachers with ECERS is about observing and giving feedback based on the data gathered. As noted earlier, the reflective cycle incorporates a pre-observation meeting to build relationship and discuss the focus of the observation (see Appendices A.1 and A.2 for the "Coach's Information Form" and "Group or Individual Coaching Questions") as well as post-observation goal setting. The feedback conference is key to impacting change.

KEY CONSIDERATIONS IN EFFECTIVE FEEDBACK

- Feedback is most potent when given in a timely manner; however, it is important to also be able to suspend judgment as you learn more about the teacher and the children enrolled.

- The opposite of caring is indifference. In the early childhood field we tend to be nice, nurturing, and caring. Because of this, some coaches tend to minimize or avoid sharing negative feedback because they don't want to be *mean* or appear picky. When we care about teachers and young children, we need to demonstrate our caring by sharing feedback on both the good and the areas needing improvement.
- Feedback means maintaining an objective focus on behavior and tangibles. Taking good notes, including actual quotes of the adults and teachers, allows us to be both specific and fact-based.
- Check for understanding. Discuss, share, ask questions, and above all *listen*. Invite teachers to restate the feedback about a specific Item, subscale, or improvement strategy to ensure they understand meaning and action.
- Validate with an "I notice" statement. These statements help to open dialog by encouraging teachers to clarify as the coach tunes into the teacher's understanding and feelings. For example, "I noticed that there were five incidents in the block area that required your intervention." Or "I noticed that you spend a total of 35 minutes in the book area during free play, reading to individual children." Or "I noticed that no children went to the nature/science center."
- Keep the discussion focused on teaching and learning.
- Identify and readily share assets you observed in the classroom. Great coaches are great encouragers. Real relationships and trust are rarely built when the coach operates with a stance of negativity. Look for the positives in what you saw, and include specific feedback on moments of effectiveness. Use the assets to build improvement in other areas.
- Be clear about what you want to accomplish with the teacher. Be realistic in what change is feasible in a specific time frame. There will always be Items out of the teacher's or coach's control. Focus on what can actually be changed, modified, or fine-tuned.
- Establish clear next steps and goals. Who will do what and when?

CONSTRUCTIVE SUPPORT

- Coach to the *head* (think, analyze, and be logical) and *heart* (feelings, emotions, intuition, and creativity). By tapping into both the head and heart, coaches develop deeper relationships with teachers, and teachers feel they are heard.
- Set goals *with* teachers, not *for* them.
- Do focused observations based on various subscales of ECERS. Although the initial observation may be a complete 3-hour observation

(in ECERS-R additional time is needed for interview), subsequent coaching observations should be shorter and focused on the specific goals established.

- Model specific strategies and discuss the teacher's observation of your modeling.
- Individualize follow-up with teachers. Recognize teachers have their own interests, needs, and stages of teacher development.
- Provide targeted professional development. Small-group meetings/workshops on areas of common concern help teachers to share with one another as they learn new strategies.
- Share and locate resources. Collect found materials; look for beautiful junk; share websites and articles; discuss with administrators materials needing to be purchased for specific classrooms as well as potential sources for donations. Hold "make and take" workshops to supplement classroom materials and activities.

STRENGTHS-BASED COACHING

As coaches, we often work from a place of trying to fix the weaknesses in teachers and the low ECERS Items, rather than from a place of capabilities and strengths (Elias, Zins, Gracyk, & Weissberg, 2003). Shifting our focus from teachers to the benefits of high-quality classrooms for children helps to take the glare off the teacher as heightened awareness of practice is reached.

Strengths-based coaching (Jablon, Dombro, & Johnsen, 2016) focuses coaching on strengths of the teacher; this is accomplished by engaging in discussion of child outcomes and what the child is experiencing. Coaches support teachers in exploring the whys of effective practices. For example, a coach may say, "I noticed the children in the block area engaged in conversation about how to make their building taller without falling down. Their conversation helps them learn about problem solving. Why do you suppose that happened?" (Pause for discussion.) After a back and forth, share another observation of an effective strategy the teacher used. "I noticed that as you overheard their conversation, you pointed to the photo of the ESB and two others photos and invited them to think. I'm curious about the question you posed: 'What's the same about the buildings in the photos?' What prompted you to intervene? And what were you hoping children would notice?"

Strengths-based coaching begins with noticing effective practices and how they support learning and from there, inviting teachers to reflect on ways to strengthen their practice.

Continuing with the vignette, a coach may say, "I noticed that some of the children were engaged in storytime this morning. Why do you think they were so engaged? I also noticed that others seemed to be more interested in each other or materials on the shelves. Why do you suppose their interest waned? (or why might they have been less engaged?)" Pause for discussion. Then: "Let's think about what you might add . . ."

Encouraging teacher metacognition means scaffolding teachers to reflect and discuss their internal thoughts and intentionality in their practice. By talking about the "*what* and *how*" and "*why*," teachers grow in being more intentional in their interactions and behavior.

WHERE TO BEGIN

Although it seems obvious, in order to effectively use ECERS as a coaching tool, you need to not only be familiar with the instrument but also know the instrument well. The Environmental Rating Scales Institute (ERSI) (www.ersi .info/training_online.html) offers introductory online training in each of the instruments. Teachers College Press also offers video training in ECERS-R (www.tcpress.com/search?search_term=ECERS). These trainings provide an overview of the scales, detailed guidance in the scoring system, and selected vignettes to practice scoring a few Items, as well as varied exercises and definitions to become more familiar with the instrument. ERSI also provides face-to-face training with practice observations as well as additional reliability observations with ERS authors and ERSI staff. Although it is not always feasible for every coach to attend such face-to-face trainings, getting reliable with a reliable rater in your state (ideally one who holds anchor status) is another option.

Once a coach is intimately familiar and preferably reliable in the administration of the instrument, we recommend completing an initial ECERS-3 or ECERS-R classroom observation or reviewing scores by a reliable rater for the individual classroom. This provides the big picture of the strengths and areas needing improvement based on the ECERS Items. Sharing the complete results, particularly with novice teachers or those with particularly low scores, can be overwhelming for teachers and is not recommended.

Coaching by subscale is more manageable for making changes as well as building the teacher's confidence and knowledge of the subscales, and implementation of improved practice. In both ECERS-3 and ECERS-R the subscales of Space and Furnishing, Personal Care Routines, followed by Program Structure are places to begin. Although many ECERS Items interact with each other throughout the scale, addressing these three subscales first provides the groundwork for the environment, including classroom space, health, and safety as well as structure of routines and schedule. These are also often the least threatening for teachers as they aren't as focused on teaching process, interactions, and content. Group support and training to introduce teachers to each subscale (beginning with these three) can be spaced out over time (at least 3 to 4 weeks apart). This affords teachers the opportunity to delve into one subscale at a time, to better understand its impact on children and objective best practice for each Item. In between these overviews, effective coaches provide individual technical assistance on the subscale being discussed, using the reflective cycle to frame goals, observations, feedback, and reflection.

Effective coaches use ECERS to engage teachers in the coaching relationship. To effect change, teachers need to see the need for the change (benefits to children), have opportunities for choice in what they work on, and understand the steps to accomplish the desired change. Using a strengths-based approach to coaching engages teachers by incorporating their interests and assets. They are an integral part of the process of growth. One's ability to engage in forward thinking is generated from one's faith, hope, and ability to reflect.

REFLECTION

The purpose of coaching is to impact the quality of classrooms for children. Benefits to children must be at the forefront of coaching. ECERS establishes a vision of quality and provides a tool to focus coaching efforts.

As often stated by the ECERS authors (Harms, Cryer, Clifford, and Yazejian), ECERS addresses the three basics of quality classrooms for young children:

- Protection of their health and safety
- Supportive interactions that foster social and emotional development and build positive relationships with adults and children
- Opportunities for activities and materials that support and extend children's learning from experience and stimulate curiosity

---

Coaching involves giving feedback and constructive support within the framework of strengths-based coaching model. This means working with the teachers' and/or director's strengths, goals, experiences, and ways of learning. Strengths-based coaching encompasses developing the adult's ability to reflect on what is going well and why what she is doing is benefiting children, as well as reflecting on what objective observations reveal needs modification. Using the ECERS subscales and Items helps to identify strengths and make change more manageable. When coaches use ECERS to link strengths and improvements to the benefits for children, a shared vision of quality becomes transparent.

Part II

COACHING WITH ECERS SUBSCALES

CHAPTER 4

Using the Subscales

Why use ECERS as a coaching tool? Higher ECERS scores lead to better child outcomes. ECERS serves as an objective measure of quality based on sound research. Using ECERS to frame coaching means that improvements benefit children in multiple ways and that coaching to higher quality can be objective. It's not making change for the sake of change, or random coaching, or coaching ambiguously. It's about using best practice to benefit children.

OVERVIEW

With a total of 35 Items in ECERS-3 or 43 Items in ECERS-R, it is impractical and overwhelming to expect to give feedback on that many Items or for a teacher or program to make change in so many different areas. By using the subscales, we are able to focus our observation and coaching on one subscale at a time. Focusing on one subscale at a time also allows teachers and administrators to be more involved in reflection and growth by targeting that subscale. Each of the next six chapters focuses on one subscale. Each chapter is framed in the same format and includes key differences between ECERS-R and ECERS-3. All strategies can be used by coaches whose role is defined by working with teachers and with directors as coaches in their work toward improvement. Coaches who work with state or county QRIS or for resource and referral agencies can coach the director or administrator in using the tools and strategies presented. This is often a more efficient approach as it builds on-site capacity of the program leader and reduces the impact of staff turnover.

- *Benefits for Children* briefly outlines the "what and why" of the subscale.
- *Quick and Easy Fixes* address practices that coaches and teachers can focus on together. Coaches who coach directors can coach administrators in tackling these areas with teachers. These are generally structural improvements that are straightforward and relatively simple to make. Some Items need administrative support, as improvement is out of the control of a classroom teacher. In

these instances, coaches need to work with the director to examine improvements that are possible. They can be addressed in a day, week, or within a month.

- *Pathways to Change over Time* includes more complex areas for ongoing coaching to make lasting improvement. These are designed for the individual who coaches classroom teachers and can also provide suggestions to coaches who coach directors in coaching teachers.
- *Fine-Tuning* involves nuances that can support already good scoring Items. Again, these are designed for the individual who coaches classroom teachers and can also provide suggestions to coaches who coach directors in coaching teachers.
- *Ideas and Hands-On Activities for Group Meetings, PLCs, and Workshops* provides suggestions for group learning, discussion, and growth. These are recommendations for the coach and/or director in their work with groups of teachers.
- *ECERS Planning Sheet* is a coaching form to complete with the teacher to outline the strengths of the classroom for the subscale as well as materials needed and practical plans for improvement, identifying a timeline as well as responsibility. The planning sheet should be completed with specific and doable steps to ensure the likelihood of change.

Based on teacher needs and interests, as well as the stage of the teacher, coaches can apply this multilayered approach to their work with teachers. Coaches working with directors can use this approach to support the director's coaching with teachers. By resolving the easy Items first, the basics are addressed to lay the foundation for more involved and often multifaceted growth and improvement. Change in practice takes time and ongoing support. Once a subscale is determined to be a focus, it is recommended that the coach spend time reviewing the subscale Items in-depth with the administrator, the teacher, or a group of teachers, with emphasis on the benefits to children. It is through understanding the "*what* and *why*" that the "*how*" can be addressed.

DIFFERENCES BETWEEN ECERS-3 AND ECERS-R

ECERS-3 is the first major revision of ECERS-R since 2005. It was updated to reflect research on best practice and includes updated content and administration. Similar to ECERS-R, it comprehensively measures overall global quality in the preschool and kindergarten classroom. Having used ECERS-R for many, many years, and ECERS-3 since its release in 2014, I have found

ECERS-3 to be a stronger scale because of its inclusion of more detail in math and literacy, as well as its emphasis on not simply having materials but on the interactions to support learning. Young children learn not only through having access to a variety of materials and playing with other children but through interactions with intentional adults.

ECERS-3 relies on a 3-hour observation on which to base assessment, whereas ECERS-R also involves a teacher interview to arrive at scores. Teachers' self-reporting, however well-intentioned, is not always accurate. For example, in asking a teacher about staff orientation and training that she received, the teacher responded only that she had gone to a workshop through her local AEYC chapter; she wasn't considering the monthly staff development sessions in her district as training. Another very honest teacher, when asked on a rainy day about the playground use, responded: "Do you want me to tell you what I'm supposed to say, or what really happens?" Sometimes teachers who are very familiar with ECERS-R and the interview questions—in the interest of getting a higher score—may be tempted to give the *correct* answer as opposed to the *real* experience for children. ECERS-3 takes the onus off teachers' knowledge of the interview questions and places it on the observed experiences of children. As we move into the subscale chapters (Chapters 5–10), specific differences in each subscale are noted. Below is a list of some of the key changes in ECERS-3.

Key changes in ECERS-3 include:

- More emphasis on interactions and the teacher's role.
- Decreased emphasis on counting materials, and more on how they are used in teaching activities.
- Greater reliance on observation of ongoing classroom activity.
- Elimination of teacher interview.
- Elimination of Parents/Staff subscale to allow more time to focus on actual classroom practices.
- Utilization of current research to determine where the Indicators lie on the spectrum of quality (improved scaling).
- Increased emphasis on engaging language, literacy, and math experiences with many new Items and Indicators.
- Distinction between *play areas* and *interest centers*.

Both ECERS-R and ECERS-3 focus on the overall global quality of a preschool or kindergarten classroom, and both follow the same scoring format. In ECERS-3, areas were shifted to reflect increased focus on matters that impact child outcomes. ECERS-3 is focused exclusively on what is observed and includes a greater emphasis on interactions and the teacher's role. Using the ECERS subscales and Items helps to identify strengths and make change more manageable. When coaches use ECERS to link strengths and improvements to the benefits for children, a shared vision of quality becomes transparent.

CHAPTER 5

Coaching to Support Space and Furnishings

This subscale addresses the areas of indoor and outdoor space and equipment, furnishings, room arrangement, display, and space for privacy. Some of these Items are out of a teacher's or coach's control. For example, the size of a room can't be changed without renovations such as knocking down walls—not practical in most centers. In addition, teachers or coaches can't move the outdoor space closer to the classroom or create one where none exists. However, there are many Items and Indicators in the subscale that can be improved to influence the quality of the indoor and outdoor environments to ensure the best environment for children. This subscale examines the many structural elements of the environment necessary for quality.

KEY SUBSCALE DIFFERENCES IN ECERS-3 AND ECERS-R

- Furnishings for relaxation and comfort (ECERS-R) is incorporated in other Items (ECERS-3) and is no longer a stand-alone Item.
- Adjustments made in scoring in gross motor equipment (time requirement and amount of appropriate equipment adjusted).

BENEFITS TO CHILDREN

Children thrive in an environment that has been designed for them and reflects them (Curtis & Carter, 2015). As such, they need ample space and equipment both inside and outside to move around freely and explore. They need child-sized chairs and tables, and appropriate storage for materials and belongings. A classroom with defined interest centers allows children to be able to access materials freely, with clear intent on the type of play encouraged in that specific area. Additionally, cozy areas that are protected from active play and have substantial soft furnishings will allow children the opportunity to lounge, daydream, read, or play quietly.

Figure 5.1. ECERS Planning Sheet

Teacher: School/Center: Coach:

DATE: Additional Info:

Space and Furnishings	Subscale score: ___
STRENGTHS	

	Who Is Responsible?	Time Frame
Materials needed		
Practical improvement plans		

Notes:

Note: A full-size printable version of this Planning Sheet is available for free download at tcpress.com/coaching-with-ecers-9780807759547

As you work with the teacher, use the ECERS Planning Sheet (see Figure 5.1) to note areas of strength and those that need improvement.

QUICK AND EASY FIXES

- Based on ECERS safety Items, work with the teacher or director to make a list of repairs or cleaning needed in the room or to furniture as well as playgrounds or equipment. The director is responsible for making repairs or arranging for them as needed.
- Teachers should be advised to clear out clutter; clutter limits the space available and can make a room seem much smaller than it is. If needed, the coach or director can assist.
- The coach and teacher should ensure that tables and chairs are child-sized for the children enrolled. Child-sized means that when a child is sitting back in the chair, her feet touch the ground, her knees fit comfortably under the table, and tables are about elbow height. Raise or lower tables as needed. Swap chairs with other classrooms as appropriate or place an order with director if necessary.
- The coach works with the teacher to focus on room arrangement to ensure clear pathways and separation between noisy and quieter centers.

- The coach helps the teacher to identify which centers are play areas and which are interest centers. Item 3 (ECERS-3) requires at least five well-defined interest centers for a score of 5. Item 4 (ECERS-R) requires at least three interest centers for a score of 5 and five interest centers for a score of 7.
- The coach works with the teacher to adjust the schedule to ensure that mornings (3-hour block including one meal) have at least 30 minutes of outdoor gross motor time (weather permitting) and at least 1 hour of indoor free play time. Children should be going outside most days year-round unless there is active precipitation or public warnings of extremely cold or hot temperatures. Although some schools may set their own particular high or low temperature when children shouldn't go outside, this is contrary to ECERS and medical professionals who value the health benefits of fresh air outside.
- The teacher and director should look at the children's cubbies. Two children in the same group should not share a cubby. In addition, to prevent spread of germs, coats and belongings from one cubby should not be touching the neighboring belongings. At a minimum, add and spread apart additional hooks as needed to store coats.
- Advise the teacher to remove any display that is dated (over a month) and/or inappropriate for the age and development of the children.
- The coach discusses the need for soft spaces, and the teacher and director may need to add pillows, rugs, and soft furnishings to create a cozy space. The cozy space can be a separate interest center or more often within the reading interest center. Solicit bean bag chairs, floor pillows, soft arm chairs (or a couch if space allows) from families, neighbors, friends, and board members. Someone may be moving or may have purchased new furniture or a rug; he can donate soft, clean items to enhance the space.

PATHWAY TO CHANGE OVER TIME

Coaches should follow up with teachers to:

- Remove items that don't support the focus of the block area, dramatic play area, nature/science area, cozy area, or defined reading interest center. This subscale requires five interest centers including a cozy area. In later Items in the scales, these are required to be well-defined interest centers, not play areas.
- Where is the space for privacy? Explore options for a space for one or two children to play without interruption.
- Focus on child-related displays. Ensure most of display is at children's eye level. At least one-third of the display should be

children's individualized work, meaning the children chose either the subject or the material used. Having 13 orange paper pumpkins with black triangle shapes glued on is *not* individualized work as it means that the teacher selected the topic (pumpkins) and the materials (orange paper and black shapes) even if the child decided how many and where to place the shapes.

- In smaller classrooms, look for ways to make better use of space, including mounting easels or book displays on walls to free up floor space. Remove any unnecessary furniture. What tables can serve dual use for meals as well as for play?

FINE-TUNING

- In rooms with windows without shades or blinds, the coach should discuss options with the teacher to enlist a volunteer to make lightweight curtains or shades to control natural light if needed.
- Work with the teacher to examine room arrangement again to ensure blocks and dramatic play or popular areas have more space. Avoiding a perimeter arrangement in favor of a grid arrangement can help with this.
- Discuss with the teacher how children know that the space for privacy has a no-interruption rule. Ensure it is enforced.
- Give feedback to the teacher about her use of display following observations (ECERS-3). Discussions during routines such as calendars or children's choice boards are not considered informal conversations about displays.
- Discuss with the teacher and director the need to secure portable gross motor equipment to encourage different skills as well as more advanced age-appropriate skills. Where can this be stored? How can staff ensure accessibility outdoors?

IDEAS AND HANDS-ON ACTIVITIES FOR GROUP MEETINGS, PLCs, AND WORKSHOPS

1. Watch the YouTube video called *Setting Up the Environment*. Pause at varying points to discuss the key concepts of the video clip (www .youtube.com/watch?v=blDMnUVbm8g&feature=youtu.be).
2. Group visualization: What is your favorite store to shop in? Brainstorm what makes this a great environment for shopping (organized shelves; easy to find what you are looking for; helpful but not intrusive sales help; not crowded; attractive displays; like items grouped together, etc.). Now what is your least favorite store

to shop in? Brainstorm why this environment doesn't work well for you (difficult to find what you want or need; hard to reach items; cluttered; crowded; loud music blasting; bothersome sales help or no one to help; items are jumbled; while you might get a good deal, you really have to search through to find your size; you end up settling for something that is okay but not really what you want, etc.). Compare the two lists. How does this relate to your classroom environment? Would you like to be a student in your room?

3. Take the group outside to the gross motor space during a nap time meeting (can also be repeated another time with indoor gross motor space). Encourage the staff to play with the equipment and materials there for about 15 minutes. Come back together and identify what gross motor skills were supported during their play. Were they able to experience at least 7–10 different skills? What could be added?

4. Prior to meeting, take photos of varying centers in classrooms and print out 8 × 10 pictures. Review the definition of interest centers (ECERS-3, p. 11; ECERS-R, p. 15) with the group. Distribute the photos and identify in small groups which were *interest centers* and which were *play centers* and why. How could a play center be adapted to be an interest center?

5. Create gross motor station bags with portable gross equipment to use in the classroom or indoor gross motor space during inclement weather. Establish a system for sharing and creating additional bags.

6. Review the playground schedule for the center. Based on space and equipment, how many classrooms can use the space at the same time *and* ensure that children are engaged, have choices, and are not crowded or waiting to use equipment? How can the schedule be adapted to ensure at least 30 minutes of outdoor gross motor time for each classroom during the morning hours. Brainstorm solutions.

7. Pair teachers to visit each other's classrooms to identify which areas are play centers and which are defined interest centers. Share findings/suggestions for room arrangement.

REFLECTION

This subscale focuses on many of the structural elements of classrooms necessary for quality. By having appropriate space and furnishings, children benefit by developing self-confidence, engagement in play, organizational skills, gross motor skills, and learning in all centers. This includes having enough space to move freely among well-defined interest centers and play areas; equipment and furnishings that are designed for young children; spaces to take a break from the pressures of other children, and to provide the softness and comfort for relaxation; and gross motor space to run freely and challenge themselves on appropriate equipment to stimulate a variety of skills.

Addressing the strengths, assets, and needs of space and furnishings is the area many coaches begin with first to lay the foundation for high-quality classrooms. It's also necessary to recognize that short of major renovation and/or expense, not all Items can be enhanced, but coaches, directors, and teachers need to work with what exists to make the best of each classroom.

CHAPTER 6

Coaching to Support Personal Care Routines

This subscale addresses meals and snacks, toileting/diapering, and health and safety practices. In this subscale, ECERS considers the extent to which staff know, follow, and consistently adhere to proper procedures. Meals should be well-balanced, provide a pleasant social atmosphere, and encourage child independence and self-help skills. There should be many conversations during mealtimes, and staff should sit with the children. Sanitary conditions are maintained for toileting with provisions convenient and accessible for children and pleasant staff-child interactions. Procedures are used to ensure a safe and healthy environment including proper handwashing for children and adults, and no more than two major safety hazards. Effective teachers understand that personal care routines are especially important in group settings.

KEY SUBSCALE DIFFERENCES IN ECERS-3 AND ECERS-R

- Greeting/departing has been eliminated.
- Nap/rest is no longer a stand-alone Item; it is now incorporated within Health Practices.
- Broader range of credit given in the 3's level; now credit can be given if at least 75% of the children have the required components for the meal and snack observed.
- Scoring has been adjusted for sanitary conditions: Level 3 = some attempt; Level 5 = usually followed (75%); Level 7 = most of the time.
- Safety Practices: Major versus minor hazards are better defined and more examples are given.
- Indoor/outdoor hazards previously combined have now been separated: Indicator 3.1 = no more than three major hazards in the outdoor environment; Indicator 3.2 = no more than three major hazards in the indoor environment; Indicator 5.1 = no more than two major hazards present (indoors and outdoors combined).
- Health Practices: If children consistently and independently complete most hygiene procedures correctly, with no staff input, credit is given

---

at the 5 level (previously it was the 3 level) since it is obvious that children have been taught to do so.
- ECERS-3 is more forgiving than ECERS-R in this subscale as credit is given at the 3 level in ECERS-3 for some attempt being made to meet health and sanitary requirements.

Figure 6.1. ECERS Planning Sheet

Teacher:	School/Center:	Coach:
DATE:	Additional Info:	

Personal Care Routines	Subscale score: ___
STRENGTHS	

	Who Is Responsible?	Time Frame
Materials needed		
Practical improvement plans		

Notes:

Note: A full-size printable version of this Planning Sheet is available for free download at tcpress.com/coaching-with-ecers-9780807759547

As you work with the teacher, use the ECERS Planning Sheet (see Figure 6.1) to note areas of strength and those that need improvement.

BENEFITS TO CHILDREN

Few would argue that ensuring the health and safety of young children is a foundational element of good preschool classrooms. Attention to health and safety practices ensures that risks are minimized and the environment limits the spread of germs and illness. In addition, children learn to follow good health practices. To minimize the spread of germs, staff should ensure that proper handwashing is carried out when required (upon arrival in class/reentry from outdoors; after play in sand or play with messy dry materials; before/after water play or use of shared moist materials—playdoh; after dealing with bodily fluids or skin contact with open sores; after touching contaminated objects). For more information on specific steps for hand-washing, you can refer to the supplemental ECERS-3 resources located at www.ersi .info/ecers3_supmaterials.html. Following these steps carefully can ensure a sanitary setting. This subscale is supported by recommendations and standards of the American Academy of Pediatrics (2011).

QUICK AND EASY FIXES

The coach works with the teacher and administrator as appropriate to:

- Ensure all bathrooms and sinks have soap, toilet paper, and paper towels easily accessible to children and that there is an effective procedure for replenishing as needed.
- Examine the daily routine and adjust as needed so no child goes more than 3 hours without eating.
- Review menus to confirm that meals follow USDA guidelines (www.ersi.info/PDF/Revised%20USDA%20Meal%20Guidelines% 20for%20ERS.pdf). Note that these were revised in October 2017. When meals are provided by parents, prepare and send home a *Good Advice Sheet* that provides varied suggestions (taking into account cultural preferences) for breakfast, lunch, and snacks that meet USDA guidelines. Arrange for the school to provide supplements when needed. Having milk on hand as well as carrot sticks, crackers, and cheese helps to meet the criteria. Send home the *Good Advice Sheet* with a note in the child's lunch box whenever components are missing, highlighting the component missing. Parents often need reminding.
- Review table washing procedures (www.ersi.info/PDF/Table%20 washing%20handout%20revised%202-11.pdf) with all staff in the classroom. Post in large print by cleaning supplies until it becomes habit. Toss out any sponges or towel rags in the classroom.
- Review major and minor safety hazards (see Appendix D, "Determining Major and Minor Hazards") present in the environment with the director and encourage the director to correct those that can be completed easily and complete maintenance requests for those that need outside assistance. ECERS-R requires that poisons be locked and out of reach of children. ECERS-3 considers poisons that are high and out of reach of children a minor hazard, but locking them up negates the hazard.
- Help the teacher develop a nap placement chart to ensure a minimum of 18 inches between cots/naps, preferably 3 feet whenever possible.

Ensure that bedding is stored so that sleeping surfaces and bedding don't touch those of another child.

PATHWAY TO CHANGE OVER TIME

- Assist the teacher in establishing routines for meals and snacks to encourage children to help with the routine (setting the table, serving themselves with child-friendly utensils, etc.).
- During a classroom observation, focus on how many times the adults in the classroom wash their own hands. Review the requirements for adult handwashing and give feedback. Keep this up until adults wash hands correctly and often as habit. Using gloves does not mean teachers don't need to wash hands first and after.
- Promote a relaxed atmosphere during meals by reviewing and revising procedures with the teaching staff to streamline setup, service, and cleanup.
- Brainstorm with the teacher quick short games and songs to engage children while waiting to use the bathroom, waiting when a meal is late arriving, or waiting for their turn to wash hands or brush teeth.
- Encourage the teachers to create a rotating playground safety checklist to regularly check for hazards.

FINE-TUNING

- Although licensing requirements in some states do not allow the use of an alcohol-based hand sanitizer in preschool and kindergarten classrooms, ECERS-3 does allow this practice only when hands are not visibly soiled and when specific sanitizer directions are followed. Particularly when bathrooms/sinks are not located in classrooms, and when allowed by your state, this can help cut down on time for washing hands particularly before meals. Explore safe storage and use with the teacher.
- Suggest topics for discussion during mealtimes to extend vocabulary and support language and social development.

IDEAS AND HANDS-ON ACTIVITIES FOR GROUP MEETINGS, PLCs, AND WORKSHOPS

1. Table Washing Procedures: It continues to surprise me when completing an ECERS observation, the number of classrooms that still don't wash and sanitize tables properly. This is not a hard thing

to do. Make up file cards that list the steps, and invite staff to put them in order. Although it's true in ECERS-3 that a classroom can score a 4 in Meals/Snacks (assuming other Indicators are met), as ECERS-3 allows for "some attempts" at the 3 level, this Item is completely under teacher control and should easily reach higher levels. Review the steps; provide materials at a meeting to make signs for classrooms.

2. Watch the YouTube video called *Handwashing and Basic Health Considerations for the Assessment Process*. Pause at varying stopping points to discuss and comment. The video is just over 13 minutes and addresses not only handwashing but also table washing (www.youtube.com/watch?v=cIkHWPW54jQ).

3. Provide materials for a make and take activity for picture/word reminders and instructions for required health practices. Use photos of children doing each step, or create or draw simple pictures to accompany the words.

4. Go to the playground and do a hunt for any major or minor hazards. Brainstorm how these can be eradicated.

5. Pair teachers to do safety checks in each other's classrooms. Our eyes often become blind to hazards in familiar settings.

REFLECTION

Personal care routines protect the health and safety of children in group settings and also help to build safe and healthy habits in young children. Although no environment can be 100% safe and healthy for a group of young children, the focus of this subscale is to minimize the dangers and accidents, ensure nutritional needs are met, and reduce the spread of germs. Many of these Items can be improved by developing safe and healthy habits in the teaching staff.

CHAPTER 7

Coaching to Support Language and Literacy

This subscale focuses on the ways that teachers support language growth and literacy development (ECERS-3) or language development and reasoning skills (ECERS-R) in the preschool and kindergarten classroom. Both scales promote vocabulary, reasoning, and informal language. They also both recognize the value of accessible, appropriate books and of adults reading to children. This subscale in ECERS-3 also encompasses emergent literacy supports for reading and writing. Regardless of the tool being used, a comprehensive intentional approach to literacy is vital.

> **KEY SUBSCALE DIFFERENCES IN ECERS-3 AND ECERS-R**
>
> In ECERS-R this subscale is called Language and Reasoning; in ECERS-3, it has been changed to Language and Literacy including five new Language and Literacy Items:
>
> - Helping children to expand vocabulary—What staff talk about is important!
> - Encouraging children to use language—We want them to talk!
> - Staff use of books with children—Are children engaged?
> - Encouraging children's use of books—Do children show interest?
> - Becoming familiar with print—Identifying letters is not enough!

As you work with the teacher, use the ECERS Planning Sheet (see Figure 7.1) to note areas of strength and those that need improvement.

BENEFITS TO CHILDREN

Vocabulary is an essential part of learning to read fluently as well as learning complex concepts (Hamre, Hatfield, Pianta, & Jamil, 2013). Research has

Figure 7.1. ECERS Planning Sheet

Teacher:	School/Center:	Coach:
DATE:	Additional Info:	

Language and Literacy	Subscale score: ___
STRENGTHS	

	Who Is Responsible?	Time Frame
Materials needed		
Practical improvement plans		

Notes:

Note: A full-size printable version of this Planning Sheet is available for free download at tcpress.com/coaching-with-ecers-9780807759547

consistently confirmed that the number of words a child knows is a strong predictor of reading success (National Early Literacy Panel, 2008). If we're going to help children build rich vocabularies, we must use lots of interesting words with them (Collins, 2014). By introducing interesting words in context, and defining or making the meaning clear, teachers are intentionally expanding vocabulary through children's play and interests. "By adding fanciful language to daily routines and conversations, teachers can help expand their thinking skills, vocabulary, and creativity as they describe the world in new ways" (Seplocha & Strasser, 2009, p. 4).

Most children are naturally curious about the world, and acting on it is how they come to know and understand. Just as they learn about oral language by exploring through listening and talking, children learn about writing by exploring through observing others to write and through teachers' encouragement of emergent writing (Schickedanz & Collins, 2013). Lastly, for children to reap the multiple benefits of daily read alouds, teachers need to maintain children's engagement and expand upon the read aloud through asking questions to support understanding and imagination (Seplocha, 2017).

QUICK AND EASY FIXES

- Discuss with the teacher ways to supplement display in the classroom with visible print combined with pictures. This is not to say one should label each and every item in the classroom; rather print should serve a purpose (what purpose does labeling a window serve?). For example, label manipulatives with print and a catalog photo of the object to help children learn what goes in which container and where to put the container. Help the teacher to make a child-friendly schedule of the daily routine in words and with photos of the child(ren) in various parts of the day (morning meeting, meals, choice time, small group, gross motor, etc.).

- Based on observation, ensure printed names of children are visible and used in the classroom. The coach should inform the teacher to add as needed.
- Discuss with the teacher ways to augment the artwork/charts to include written comments by writing/transcribing what the child dictates as caption or experience story.
- The coach and teacher should make certain that there are *minimally* at least 15 books accessible to children in the reading interest center. The actual number depends on the total amount of children in the class; *many books* means at least 35 books for 20 children. Although there may be books available in other centers that support the reading interest center, this center needs to be a well-defined one.
- The coach informs the teacher to remove any books that may be frightening, in poor shape, or that promote a negative stereotype or social message. This includes many traditional fairy tales where characters eat, bully, or kill another character, as well as stories with guns, depicting Indians as savages, or with other negative implications.

PATHWAY TO CHANGE OVER TIME

- Reading a story aloud that no one listens to, is too long, is read without expression, or that is interrupted by the teacher's handling of class management is frankly a waste of time and not engaging for children. For teachers who have difficulty maintaining children's interest during whole-group read aloud, coaches should help the teacher to reframe the read aloud time by dividing the group in two and having read aloud be in small groups with each adult reading a story to his own group. These teachers may also benefit by observing a read aloud with a skilled, engaging teacher.
- Discuss with the teacher and ask her to add to various centers and places writing materials that are appropriate to the function of the center. For example, add file cards and markers to make signs for block buildings; add post-it notes and recipe cards to the dramatic play center to take phone messages, make shopping lists, or jot

down a recipe being "cooked"; bring outside file cards and markers to be able to give a speeding ticket to a child going too fast on the tricycle.
- Observe and give feedback to the teacher on ways she can enhance her interactions with children to extend their language use and vocabulary.

FINE-TUNING

- Encourage the teacher to use a local library to supplement the class library, ensuring at least five books are accessible that relate to the current theme or classroom activities.
- Brainstorm practical strategies for obtaining books for the classroom. For example, in one school, the teachers discourage parents from purchasing decorations and plates for a classroom birthday party; instead they encourage parents to donate a book from their wish list to the classroom library and label the inside cover with *Celebrating [child's name] Birthday* and the date.
- The coach and teacher should examine classroom books and discuss ways the teacher can supplement as needed to ensure a wide selection of books of varied genres including books depicting differing abilities, different cultures and races, nontraditional gender roles, and children's feelings. Include books about various topics such as health, jobs/work, males and females, math, factual items, nature/science, people, sports/hobbies, and any topics of interest and relevance to the children.
- Discuss classroom opportunities to support phonological awareness that support children hearing the sounds of letters and words in a fun and engaging way. This is not to advocate for drill and whole-group lessons but to become more playful with and aware of sounds, alliteration, and rhyme.

IDEAS AND HANDS-ON ACTIVITIES FOR GROUP MEETINGS, PLCs, AND WORKSHOPS

1. Vocabulary Explosion: Divide the group into small groups of three or four people. Assign each group a particular center or play area in the classroom, or a specific routine (meals, gross motor time, etc.). Invite the groups to brainstorm as many fanciful words as they can that relate to that center or routine. For example, the dramatic play list may include words such as spatula, colander, spice, sauté, and cutlery. Provide large flip chart paper and markers

so that teachers can select words from the lists of others to post high up in their classroom for each center or routine to remind teachers to use and define these interesting words in the course of their natural interactions with children as they play. Depending on the size of the group, this can be done over several short sessions so that adults have new vocabulary to use for each center/routine.

2. Repeat the above activity, only this time let each small group select a different theme of study and brainstorm interesting vocabulary to support the topic. Gather and type up the lists and distribute to each classroom.

3. Relational Conversations: The purpose of this activity is to encourage teachers to extend interactions beyond a simple back and forth interchange. Provide a sheet of old newspaper to each pair, and ask them to crunch it up to make a ball. Give each pair a common classroom object such as a puzzle, links, magnifying glass, or a unit block. For the activity, have each pair stand about 6 feet apart and toss the newspaper ball back and forth. As they toss the ball to their partner, they should make a comment or ask a question appropriate to the classroom object as if a child was playing with it. The person catches the ball and responds as they toss it back. Encourage them to continue the conversation for as many tosses as they can. Then change objects with another pair and repeat. When all pairs have completed at least two objects, gather the group back and process the activity. How many back and forth interchanges were you able to do? What did you talk about? Were some objects easier than others? How does this activity relate to your interactions with children?

4. Watch the YouTube video called *Intentional Teaching: Supporting Literacy*. Pause at varying points to discuss the key concepts of the video clip (www.youtube.com/watch?v=E8a_QKF8XSM&feature =youtu.be).

5. Article Share: Ask each staff member to find an article about using vocabulary with young children from a journal such as *Teaching Young Children*. At a group meeting, facilitate a sharing of the key points of the articles and how they can be applied in their classrooms.

6. Brainstorm a list of natural classroom opportunities for teachers to help children become familiar with print.

7. Invite a storyteller to visit a staff meeting to share ways he maintains children's engagement.

REFLECTION

Few would argue against developing language and literacy skills in young children. Having a strong foundation in vocabulary and emergent literacy leads to improved reading, writing, speaking, listening, and comprehension skills as children move into elementary grades. Young children don't learn letters in isolation (i.e., letter of the week) but develop literacy skills and understanding through learning in context in the course of their play and routine.

Concerns arise through trying to build these skills through rote learning, drill, extended teacher direction, the use of workbooks, and other developmentally inappropriate practices. These sometimes stem from lack of education or knowledge of how children learn to read and write, feelings of parental pressure, lack of trust in learning through engagement and play, and/or absence of the understanding of developmentally appropriate strategies to support emergent literacy skills. Adding vocabulary is key to children's literacy development. Using a wide range of vocabulary about the children's here and now (their interests and play), and stretching out the context of discussions with individuals and small groups leads to increased vocabulary. Maintaining engagement during story reading, encouraging children to engage with books, and supporting children's understanding of the form and function of print in natural ways are meaningful practices to support children's growth. Improvements in this subscale sometimes require educating staff, and time to make lasting change.

CHAPTER 8

Coaching to Support Learning Activities

The skills children develop during their early years are the cornerstone for their future growth and development. In this subscale, both ECERS-R and ECERS-3 consider that preschool and kindergarten children should have diverse, appropriate materials accessible, arranged into clearly defined interest centers and play areas that are organized for children's independent use. Also addressed in both scales is the amount of time that all children should have access to a wide variety of materials as well as the teaching and interactions that occur as children use materials. High-quality classrooms ensure that effective classroom interactions and instruction are connected to content.

KEY SUBSCALE DIFFERENCES IN ECERS-3 AND ECERS-R

- In ECERS-R, this subscale is Activities; in ECERS-3, it is Learning Activities, placing emphasis not simply on provision of materials but on teacher support and interactions when children use the materials.
- Sand/water is now incorporated into Nature/science.
- Time access to all materials has been adjusted. ECERS-R requires access for a *substantial portion of the day* (one-third of the children's day); ECERS-3 requires at least 1 hour of access during the 3-hour observation.
- Math/number has been expanded with three new math Items:
  - » Math in daily events—Not about having math materials but how math is drawn into the lives and activities of the children.
  - » Understanding written numbers—How staff introduce numbers to children in a meaningful way.
  - » Math materials and activities—Not just about access to materials, but instead about how staff use and teach with the materials in a way that engages children.

As you work with the teacher, use the ECERS Planning Sheet (see Figure 8.1) to note areas of strength and those that need improvement.

Figure 8.1. ECERS Planning Sheet

Teacher:	School/Center:	Coach:
DATE:	Additional Info:	

Learning Activities	Subscale score: ___
STRENGTHS	

	Who Is Responsible?	Time Frame
Materials needed		
Practical improvement plans		

Notes:

Note: A full-size printable version of this Planning Sheet is available for free download at tcpress.com/coaching-with-ecers-9780807759547

BENEFITS TO CHILDREN

Curriculum has many definitions as it means different things to different educators (Kostelnik, Soderman, Whiren, & Rupiper, 2015). ECERS consider curriculum holistically to include the learning environment and materials, adult-child interactions, teaching strategies, and content areas. All are interdependent and connected, and all impact the learning opportunities and outcomes for children. Although the organization and diversity of materials are important, time is equally important as it allows children to explore a variety of play materials in a supported environment. Uninterrupted blocks of time help children develop problem-solving and decision-making skills by offering a choice of activities.

When teachers circulate throughout the various centers asking questions and adding information and new words and ideas related to children's play, children thrive and learning is maximized (Englehart, Mitchell, Albers-Biddle, Jennings-Towle, & Forestieri, 2016; Tomlinson & Hyson, 2012). Children are also able to interact with their peers while expressing their creativity and imagination. Culturally diverse materials and activities help children learn that there are many different types of people in the world and also allow them to understand the similarities as well as differences that make us who we are.

In recognition of the importance of math development (Charlesworth, 2015; Erikson Institute, 2014) for preschool and kindergarten children,

ECERS-3 expanded math Items. These new Items promote children's acquisition and use of the language and vocabulary of math, conceptual understanding of math content, and children's development of perseverance and persistence in solving problems.

With the comprehensive inclusion in both scales of fine motor, art, music and movement, blocks, dramatic play, nature/science, diversity, and technology, and teachers' encouragement in the use of all centers (ECERS-3), the scales ensure that all areas of development and content are addressed in developmentally appropriate ways. Young children are more interested in the process of creating rather than in the end product. Therefore, children should be allowed to use materials flexibly with no expected product. They learn more when they select things that interest them. Hands-on active learning is an important vehicle for children's learning and development as well as a reflection of their learning development.

QUICK AND EASY FIXES

- Examine the schedule and work with the teachers to adjust as needed. For ECERS-R, this means that all required materials and centers are accessible for a substantial portion of the day as defined in ECERS-R (p. 7). For ECERS-3, this means that all required materials and centers are accessible (p. 10) for at least 1 hour during the 3-hour observation. I always recommend that teachers plan for at least 70–75 minutes for free choice as the *clock* for the hour does not begin until all children are actually playing; children's planning time is not considered part of the hour. In addition, once cleanup is called, access ends even if no one is cleaning up. The time requirements are weaved throughout the scales in multiple Items. Ensuring the required times for access, therefore, impacts scores and benefits to child significantly.
- Coaches and teachers should look for print numbers in displays accompanied by pictures that show what the number means. These can easily be added by the teacher if not present by displaying the number of children allowed in an area with dots accompanying the written number or displaying a number line with picture objects to represent the written number or using picture and number on a displayed recipe chart (e.g., 1 cup of flour, 3 tablespoons of sugar) or using slash marks with the total number on a chart of how many voted for each name for the new class pet.
- Discuss how the teacher makes sure she limits the time a child uses the computer or tablet. Discuss why this is important for children. Institute a procedure for limiting time when none was observed.
- The coach and teacher should look at how diversity is represented in this classroom. Discuss resources (families, neighborhood,

photos, library, places of worship) that the teacher can use to add enhancements as needed.

PATHWAY TO CHANGE OVER TIME

- Both ECERS-3 and ECERS-R clearly define the amount and categories of materials for many Items in the scale. Examine each center with the teacher, and make a list of what additional materials are needed to ensure categories and amounts are addressed. Although some materials may need to be purchased, many can be donated (collage materials, dress-up clothing, musical instruments, recyclable materials, wood scraps, etc.), made, or found at yard sales. Refer to Appendix C, "ECERS-3 Materials Checklist," for specifics of the individual Items.
- As needed and if allowed, brainstorm fundraising ideas and implement to raise funds to purchase needed materials.
- Based on your observations, what areas are more popular in the classroom and what areas did children not go to? What areas did the teacher neglect or not go to? Discuss ways the adults can encourage children to play in all centers.
- Focus on how creativity is supported in this classroom. Discuss the difference between product and process, and teacher-directed craft projects, and open-ended art activity.

FINE-TUNING

- Have a conversation with the teacher about what he (or you) observed his children doing or creating. Focus the discussion on what he can do to show children he is interested and to extend their learning based on specific activities/children shared.
- Encourage the teacher to write captions or encourage older children to write about their artwork. Discuss the message this gives to children.
- Focus an observation on the ways the teacher supports phonological awareness. Point out instances you observed when she pointed out rhyming words, played with rhyme and alliteration, and encouraged children to experiment with the sounds of words. Suggest ways she can incorporate this practice into her daily interactions with children.
- Discuss ways the teacher can extend learning in block play by linking writing and math concepts and words in his interactions with children in the block area and dramatic play.
- Assist the teacher in labeling containers and shelves to support self-help skills.

IDEAS AND HANDS-ON ACTIVITIES FOR GROUP MEETINGS, PLCs, AND WORKSHOPS

1. Book Discussion Group: There are many great books to use with teachers in a book club or PLC that address varying Items in this subscale. In Chapter 12, some suggestions are provided.
2. Watch the YouTube video called *Exploring Math Everyday*. Pause at varying sections to discuss key points (www.youtube.com/watch?v=KfHyxUDQCBg&feature=youtu.be).
3. Hold a make and take workshop; provide varied materials and invite teachers to bring materials as well (e.g., magazines, photos, yarn, buttons, bottle caps, and other found materials). Focus each session on one area: nature/science, math, or fine motor.
4. Go on a nature walk with the staff. Encourage staff to take photos of things they see and to collect rocks, twigs, pinecones, leaves, and other materials to bring back to their classrooms. Come back and share with each other ways they can bring nature into their room and activities. Invite staff to print out photos they took to display, and/or make a book or puzzle.
5. Go into one of the larger classrooms and have at least 30 minutes of free play for the adults. Gather back as a group and discuss what children learn from each center as well as what they did and felt. Why were some areas more popular than others?
6. Each Item in this subscale lends itself to a workshop. Lead a hands-on workshop or invite a teacher to cofacilitate the session with you. Select Items from this subscale to delve more deeply into ways they can enhance the area, ask higher-level questions, and support children's learning. Encourage staff to share resources and ideas they use.

REFLECTION

The Learning Activities subscale has more Items than the other subscales as it addresses both content and centers necessary in high-quality classrooms. Having extended periods of choice time (no less than 1 hour) with many and varied materials and teacher encouragement of play in the varied centers supports the balance of child initiation and adult facilitation or scaffolding. As children learn through their play, having time, materials, and scaffolding are keys to support and expand children's learning in all areas. Coaches should therefore address these practices first as they impact several Items. Because math and science are frequently areas in which staff need support and strategies, coaches often spend time focusing PD and individual coaching conferences on these topics.

CHAPTER 9

Coaching to Support Interaction

Interactions are at the heart of intentional teaching and are therefore naturally imbedded throughout the scale. Interactions specific to this subscale include how teachers handle discipline, support peer interactions, supervise children, and interact with children to support their learning. ECERS-3 adds particular attention to individualizing teaching and learning. Coaching in this subscale means helping teachers to use high-quality classroom interaction strategies that strengthen concept development, quality of feedback, and language modeling for children.

KEY SUBSCALE DIFFERENCES IN ECERS-3 AND ECERS-R

- General supervision has been removed in ECERS-3 and is incorporated in other Items throughout the scale. Supervision of gross motor remains in both scales.
- Both social and teaching interactions are considered throughout both scales.
- New Item in ECERS-3 on *Individualized Teaching* with more emphasis on matching teacher interactions with the children's abilities and interests to engage them. At the lowest level, teaching content is the same for all children (e.g., reciting days of the week, rote group repetition, same questions to all). At the highest level, teachers support children's learning in ways that are meaningful and developmentally appropriate.

As you work with the teacher, use the ECERS Planning Sheet (see Figure 9.1) to note areas of strength and those that need improvement. Also refer to Appendix C, "ECERS-3 Materials Checklist," for specifics of the individual Items.

Figure 9.1. ECERS Planning Sheet

Teacher:	School/Center:	Coach:
DATE:	Additional Info:	

Interaction	Subscale score: ___
STRENGTHS	

	Who Is Responsible?	Time Frame
Materials needed		
Practical improvement plans		

Notes:

Note: A full-size printable version of this Planning Sheet is available for free download at tcpress.com/coaching-with-ecers-9780807759547

BENEFITS TO CHILDREN

Although nurturing and responsive supervision of children throughout the day is of course important to ensure safety and support learning, supervision of children during gross motor activity is especially vital to not only prevent accidents but also to support gross motor skill development. Gross motor time is not a time for teachers to relax and chat with each other. When teachers remain near the most challenging equipment, they are able to stop any potentially dangerous activities and teach children how to safely and correctly use the equipment. Staff can show enthusiasm for gross motor play by organizing vigorous and active play activities, as well as helping children acquire and develop more advanced gross motor skills. Concepts (positional words, nature/science) as well as expanding vocabulary are supported through supervision of gross motor activities.

When healthy relationships exist, learning and teaching are more invigorating (Shonkoff, 2017). When this occurs, children are more invested and engaged, and in turn strive for excellence. As educators, our role is to build on their questions, inquisitiveness, curiosity, and interests, and to know when and how to scaffold their learning (Strasser & Bresson, 2017). Interested and meaningful learning goes beyond academic skills. Teaching is individualized when teachers respond to the varying abilities, needs, and interests of children in the group, modeling and discussing various concepts for children and allowing them to explore and participate in activities at their own pace and interest level. Using an individualized approach in teaching is important as it supports the wide range of skills, needs, abilities, and interests of all children in the classroom. Staff do this as they circulate around the classroom. This is a regular part of what they do.

Children develop social skills as they learn how to interact with both peers and adults. When teachers call attention to children's feelings in reactions to another student's actions, children learn that their actions affect others. For example, if a child shares playdough and the other child smiles, teachers explain that the positive action caused the other child to be happy. Adversely, if a child knocks down another child's block structure and the child cries or gets angry, the teacher explains why the child is having that reaction. This can help children to recognize verbal and nonverbal social cues and understand that their actions can have positive and negative responses. Modeling positive social behavior can show children how to interact with each other and encourages positive peer relationships. Staff can also assist children with their attempts to interact with each other by guiding them with positive feedback and close supervision.

Classroom atmospheres should be relaxed and supportive of children's ideas and feelings. This benefits children as it provides them with the foundations of supported learning and encourages them to try new things and interact positively with those around them. Staff interactions with children should be positive and respectful. The goal of effective discipline is to help children learn to manage their own behavior and develop self-regulation. Using positive approaches to discipline children allows them to maintain good self-esteem and helps them to understand why their behavior was inappropriate while being supported and encouraged to solve issues in a satisfying way. Teachers help children work out problems by asking questions and having them talk out their feelings and frustrations, which supports social and emotional development.

QUICK AND EASY FIXES

- To help children avoid conflicts throughout the day, there should be a clear system in all classrooms ensuring fair turns are given. Suggest that the teacher use a timer or waiting list for popular activities and materials to ensure all children have a chance to use materials that they are interested in. When there is a clear system in their classroom, children are more likely to be patient and wait their turn.
- If there is no gross motor activity observed during the 3-hour observation for ECERS-3, Item 28 will automatically score 1. This means even on days when weather does not permit use of the playground, children should still have the opportunity for vigorous

gross motor in the classroom if no other appropriate indoor space exists. In ECERS-R when no gross motor activity is scheduled during the observation, scoring is completed based on general supervision observed as well as teacher interview regarding how gross motor supervision occurs. The coach should discuss with teachers and administrators to ensure children go outside most every day except during active precipitation or health warnings. Ensure that on days children must remain indoors that they have at least 10 minutes (preferably more) of vigorous gross motor activity.

PATHWAY TO CHANGE OVER TIME

- Make the teacher aware of any negative physical contact or discipline strategies observed. Encourage her to share why she reacted in that manner and what a more effective positive response could be.
- Open a dialogue about why the teacher chooses to teach. What does he like about working with children, and what causes his stress?
- Review with the teacher the expectations for Individualized Teaching and Learning. Based on data collected during an observation, share with her instances when her interactions could be categorized as level 1, level 3, or level 5. Discuss strategies to support more level 3 and level 5 interactions. Levels are presented here:
  - » Level 1: Teaching content is the same for all the children (days of the week recited, writing your name, same book for all)
  - » Level 3: Staff ask children questions that they are able to answer during free play activities (identifying shapes, colors, counting)
  - » Level 5: Staff have higher-level interactions during children's activities as they circulate through the room to scaffold learning; children respond well and are successful during activities.
- Share Appendix B, "ECERS-3 List of Interactions," with the teacher. While interactions are incorporated into many Items throughout the scale, point out the variety of interactions observed as well as those missed.

FINE-TUNING

- When teachers are responsive to children and recognize their role as a facilitator of learning, to further support individualized teaching and learning, it is appropriate to help a teacher move from a level 5 to level 7. Level 7 means that most all teaching is individualized and that there is also much individualized teaching while children participate in free play. Share instances of picking up on teachable moments as well as missed opportunities. Invite a dialog about ways to individualize staff-directed activities.

- Look for nonverbal cues from child(ren), and discuss with the teacher about what children are telling him and what that means for his interactions.
- Discuss the difference between praise and encouragement. A simple Internet search for "praise versus encouragement" will lead you to a variety of short articles and excerpts should you feel you need to get a better understanding of the distinction and effects of each.

IDEAS AND HANDS-ON ACTIVITIES FOR GROUP MEETINGS, PLCs, AND WORKSHOPS

1. Being in a classroom with young children all day can be stressful. Stress can cause teachers to lose their cool, or become short-tempered, or frustrated with children. Facilitate a workshop on stress management.
2. Invite teachers to bring one new idea for gross motor activity to share with their peers. At the meeting, encourage them also to share memories of their own gross motor play as children.
3. Watch the YouTube video called *Intentional Teaching: Supporting Literacy*. Pause at varying points to discuss the ways the teachers interact with intention to expand on children's ideas, interests, and thinking (www.youtube.com/watch?v=E8a_QKF8XSM&feature=youtu.be).
4. Focus a staff meeting on sharing ways they support peer interaction throughout the day. Include ways they help children to solve social problems and opportunities for children to work on a project together. Focus on why these strategies are beneficial for children. What do children learn when teachers provide these supports and opportunities?
5. Hold a workshop on positive approaches to discipline. Provide or ask teachers to write out a brief scenario about a child or situation in their room that requires discipline. For example, one scenario may be about the block area, which seems to frequently be the location of conflicts with children's buildings getting knocked down. Another scenario may involve children who frequently disrupt morning meetings or storytime. In teams or small groups, brainstorm ways to address the situation and support children's social and emotional development.
6. Prior to a staff meeting, ask teachers to spend at least 10 minutes surfing around this website (challengingbehavior.fmhi.usf.edu). At

the staff meeting invite them to share what they read and found interesting. What was your takeaway from this website?
7. There are four free online modules on promoting social and emotional competence in preschool (csefel.vanderbilt.edu/resources /training_preschool.html). Each module provides a PowerPoint presentation, handouts, and notes for the presenter. Based on the needs and interests of your staff, select the module(s) you feel would be most appropriate.

REFLECTION

Just as relationships and interactions are vital in coaching adults, the interaction subscale focuses on the importance of adult-child interaction to support children's growth. Whether in the classroom or outside on the playground or a walk, whether during free play or daily routines, whether handling discipline or individualizing teaching and learning, what comes out of the adult's mouth can amplify children's learning. Effective coaches often use direct quotes of teacher language to point out strengths and reflect on more meaningful interactions. Helping teachers learn to capitalize on teachable moments, understand the difference between encouragement and praise, ask higher-level questions and lengthening interactions (more back and forth interchange), as well as use positive approaches to classroom management and discipline are the cornerstones of coaching in this subscale.

CHAPTER 10

Coaching to Support Program Structure

This subscale examines the structure of the classroom day. ECERS-3 and ECERS-R include similar Items in this subscale. Both expect that children have opportunities for free play. A total of at least 1 hour of free play (ECERS-3) or a substantial portion of the day (ECERS-R) including both indoor free play and outdoor gross motor free play is required for good scores. Free play means that children can select materials as well as which companions they want to play with. If children are assigned to centers or staff select groups or materials, then *this is NOT free play*. Free play requires that children have access to ample and varied materials. In addition, there is a clear system used to regulate participation in activities, such as a timer or waitlist for popular centers, equipment, or materials.

Transitions should be smooth with teachers prepared for the next activity, and children should not have to wait more than 3 minutes between activities. Whole-group activities, if offered, are limited in time, are developmentally appropriate, and engaging to children. At the highest levels, group activities are usually carried out in smaller groups (e.g., the teacher reads a story to one group of children while the teacher assistant reads a story to the other small group in a different area of the classroom), and children are allowed to leave whole-group activities to go to another area/activity that is more interesting to them.

KEY SUBSCALE DIFFERENCES IN ECERS-3 AND ECERS-R

- Schedule has been removed and is incorporated within Transitions and waiting times.
- Provisions for children with disabilities is incorporated in other Items and is no longer a stand-alone Item.

As you work with the teacher, use the ECERS Planning Sheet (see Figure 10.1) to note areas of strength and those that need improvement.

Figure 10.1. ECERS Planning Sheet

Teacher: School/Center: Coach:

DATE: Additional Info:

Program Structure	Subscale score: ___	
STRENGTHS		

	Who Is Responsible?	Time Frame
Materials needed		
Practical improvement plans		

Notes:

Note: A full-size printable version of this Planning Sheet is available for free download at tcpress.com/coaching-with-ecers-9780807759547

BENEFITS TO CHILDREN

Whenever teachers use whole-group activities for play and learning, if there are any children that have trouble participating, staff should consider doing activities in smaller groups, provide support for these children, or allow children to leave the whole-group activity to work in another area that is more satisfying to them. This will help ensure children's engagement and success while participating in whole-group activities. When possible, activities should be completed in smaller groups to allow teachers to individualize attention and maximize child engagement.

In the course of a typical preschool day there are multiple transitions as children move throughout the day. In a morning observation, children may have one or two meals, morning meetings, free choice time in centers, gross motor time, listen to stories, as well as tend to toileting and washing their hands several times. Transitions help children to follow a routine, find comfort in knowing what comes next, and learn to sequence their day. They also are learning that sometimes you have to wait. In high-quality classrooms, teachers are typically prepared for transitions and moving between different parts of the daily routine, and there are no transitions and wait times (3 minutes or longer). By avoiding long wait times for children, as well as ensuring all children are actively engaged during all wait times and transitions (i.e., singing songs, doing finger plays, playing rhyming games), learning time is maximized without long transitions and idle time.

Free play affords children the opportunity to make choices, explore, experiment, and follow their interests. The benefits of free play are well documented. As noted in the NAEYC Position Statement on Developmentally Appropriate Practice, "Play is an important vehicle for developing self-regulation as well as for promoting language, cognition, and social competence" (NAEYC, 2009, p. 14). Engaging in play, particularly sociodramatic play, is critically important for development and learning and later academic success. Marilou Hyson states that "play is not a break from learning but a pathway to learning" (Bohart, Charner, & Koralek, 2015, p. 96). Recognizing that children are active learners who learn through their play is key in establishing the schedule. Free play supports integrated learning in all domains, allowing more individualized scaffolding as staff intentionally interact following children's choices, interests, and leads.

Group activities, whether whole or small group, should be used as an extension of learning that is taking place during choice time and to strengthen connections to various content areas. Group activities should also be engaging and provide connections to children's interest and the current topic(s) being explored. Intentional teaching involves balancing child-guided experiences with adult-guided experiences to optimize learning (Epstein, 2014).

QUICK AND EASY FIXES

- Ensure the daily schedule includes at least 1 hour of free play both inside and outside during the morning. To meet Indicators in other subscale Items, the observed schedule should have a minimum of 1 hour of center time access as well as a minimum of 30 minutes of gross motor activity (ECERS-3) or a substantial portion of the day for free play and 1 hour of gross motor time (ECERS-R). Assist the teacher in making adjustments as needed.
- Free play needs to be free play. Coaches should have teachers discontinue the use of assigning children to centers, or rotating children through centers, as this is not considered to be free play. Free play means children have choices.
- Coaches and teachers should examine the daily schedule to see the number of transitions children experience in the course of a typical day. This can be particularly problematic when sinks and toilets are located outside the classroom. Look for opportunities to minimize transitions. For example, when gross motor time is followed by a meal, children can wash hands on their way back from the playground. If lunch is typically late arriving to the classroom, plan for a short storytime while waiting for lunch to arrive.

PATHWAY TO CHANGE OVER TIME

- Observe the teaching staff specifically during free play time. Chart how long they spent in each area as well as the type of interaction (e.g., managing behavior, giving information, asking low-level questions, and extended interaction). Review the data with the teacher to make her more aware of her actions and interactions during free play.
- Share songs, finger plays, rhyming, or alliteration games that can be used to minimize wait time and maintain children's engagement.
- Examine the purpose of whole groups that occur in this classroom. Although there are benefits in building class community through brief morning meetings, are there other whole group times that can be better individualized as well as more engaging if the activity is completed in small groups? Discuss this change with the teacher.
- It can be difficult to break a habit of long whole-group times as some teachers feel they are only teaching when they are in front of the group and/or children are responding in rote. Make arrangements for the teacher to observe a morning in a more appropriate classroom, and discuss differences between what he saw and what he does. Share and discuss articles about the benefits of free play. For some reluctant teachers, it may be necessary to enforce a time limit on whole-group time and discuss what parts of it she can do without.

FINE-TUNING

- Revisit the daily routine together. Are there transitions that can be completed individually or in small groups to minimize wait time? For example, if children eat breakfast immediately on arrival, children can wash their hands individually as they arrive and then sit down for breakfast, thereby meeting the requirements for two handwashing instances by one.
- Brainstorm together what materials can be added to the classroom to support exploration of the current theme or study.
- Model using interesting words with children in the classroom during free play. Inform the teacher of your purpose. Modeling is only effective if the teacher knows you are intentionally modeling and there is follow-up discussion. Meet to discuss what words you used, when, and why.

IDEAS AND HANDS-ON ACTIVITIES FOR GROUP MEETINGS, PLCs, AND WORKSHOPS

1. Start a staff meeting with three to five singalongs or other transition activities. You can provide the songs/activities or assign a couple of staff members to share a song/activity they've not seen used or heard in the school. Sing/play each a few different times during the meeting and at a subsequent meeting so the staff can add to their repertoire. This is particularly useful for newer or less experienced teachers.

2. PLC Idea: Work as a team to revisit the school's playground schedule to make adjustments where needed to ensure schedules include required time for outdoor gross motor free play.

3. Establish or reinforce a culture that values free play. Post quotes in staff restrooms, staff lounges, offices, and hallways that speak to free play. A few of my favorites accessed from www.brainyquote.com and files.eric.ed.gov/fulltext/ED440779.pdf are noted here:

   » Children have real understanding only of that which they invent themselves, and each time that we try to teach them something too quickly, we keep them from re-inventing it themselves. Jean Piaget (1896–1980)

   » If a child can't learn the way we teach, maybe we should teach the way they learn. Ignacio Estrada

   » A child's brain is a fire to be ignited, not a pot to be filled. John Locke (1632–1704)

   » Don't force a child to learn. Create a desire to want to learn. Jean-Jacque Rousseau (1712–1778)

   » Man does not cease to play because he grows old; man grows old because he ceases to play. George Bernard Shaw (1856–1950)

   » The mediocre teacher tells. The good teacher explains. The superior teacher demonstrates. The great teacher inspires. William Arthur Ward

   » Too often we give our children answers to remember rather than problems to solve. Roger Lewin

   » Wonder is the beginning of wisdom. Greek Proverb

4. Invite teachers to find an article about the benefits of free play to share with their peers. Facilitate the discussion around why free play is so important for young children.

REFLECTION

Although the Program Structure subscale has the fewest number of Items in both ECERS-3 and ECERS-R, the Items form the basis for the daily routine through schedule and free play, transitions, and whole-group activity. This subscale is often addressed earlier in coaching as the Items set the tone for the classroom. In order for benefits to children to be realized, teachers, directors, and coaches need to value free play as a primary vehicle for children's learning, as well as recognize that any whole-group activities need to be short and engaging. Coaches can also provide resources and strategies to handle and minimize transitions and wait times.

Part III

PUTTING IT ALL TOGETHER

Part II

PUTTING IT ALL TOGETHER

CHAPTER 11

Nuts and Bolts

The teacher's role in creating high-quality preschool learning environments is critical to fostering the skills needed for children to maximize their potential. Effective coaching with ECERS is grounded on using specific instances during observations to provide feedback. Effective coaching involves routinely using ECERS evidence and data to make improvements against goals. Coaches and directors support teachers in continually refining their teaching based on reflection on multiple forms of data. ECERS provides a snapshot of what occurs in a classroom on a typical day. Coaching, therefore, involves providing objective information about what was observed and making plans for more effective practices. ECERS subscales provide a way to break down the coaching process to manageable steps toward improvement. We also recommend that coaches and administrators use *All About ECERS-R* (Cryer, Harms, & Riley, 2003) to understand the nuances and requirements of each of the ECERS-R Items. *All About ECERS-3* is projected for a 2019 release.

In this chapter, we provide guidance and rationale in coaching groups and highlight the important partnership between the coach and administrator. Tips for ECERS-3 and ECERS-R are also included.

COACHING IN STAFF MEETINGS, PLCs, AND WORKSHOPS

The ability to make change directly connects to one's ability to engage in forward thinking—generated from one's knowledge and understanding of child development and learning, and ability to reflect. Engaging preschool teachers in thoughtful thinking regarding theoretical perspectives—which already drive their practice—may ignite intentional planning. Providing teachers with the opportunity to engage in professional discourse regarding their practice deepens their perspectives and understandings and incites self-reflection. Giving teachers the opportunity to hear the perspectives of their colleagues through focused group discussions can enlighten, empower, and validate them.

Continuous quality improvement means taking advantage of available time for sharing ideas, identifying strengths, problem solving, and discussing concerns. Coaches examine ECERS scoresheets to identify and celebrate common Items scoring a 5 or better. This means that developmentally appropriate practices are generally occurring in those Items being rated as good to excellent. Identifying program strengths and relating those Items to the program's vision and benefits to children help to reinforce good practice.

Although individual teachers may have specific areas needing improvement, often issues requiring change are program-wide or are observed in more than one or two classrooms within a program. These Items may best be addressed through group meetings, workshops, and/or professional learning communities. By examining ECERS scoresheets across the program, professional development can be planned to address common areas of need. Regardless of whether the workshop is facilitated by the coach, director, or outside consultant, it is important that the facilitator be familiar with the specific ECERS Item(s) that relate to that topic. For example, a workshop on discipline should focus on positive techniques for handling discipline and not include recommendations for using what ECERS considers strict or harsh forms of discipline (e.g., withholding food; withholding outdoor play time; time-out as a preferred strategy; belittling or embarrassing children by writing the misbehaviors or individuals' names on a board; and/or threatening children).

The following list shows the types of activities in which coaches can help administrators to involve their teachers in working on issues that the director deems worthy of focus:

Anatomy of a Workshop

Icebreaker or Opening Activity	Mini Lecturette (Content)
Welcome and Logistics	Active Learning Activity
Goals and Objectives	Group Process and Discussion
Mini Lecturette (Content)	Wrap-Up and Questions
Active Learning Activity	Closure/Next Steps
Group Process and Discussion	

Most programs hold staff meetings at least monthly. These are usually organized by the director or administrator to keep staff informed of upcoming events and program procedures or changes. To maximize the value of this time, we recommend providing an information sheet that can be distributed in written form via staff memos, emails, and/or postings on staff bulletin boards. This can allow for time for focused discussion on a particular ECERS Item of concern. For example, gathering staff input on a playground schedule to ensure required times for all classrooms to use the playground and/or gross motor spaces can involve staff in seeing the big picture of what is needed for all children to support vigorous active gross motor play.

Professional learning communities (PLCs) can be established to focus on specific ECERS subscales and/or Items. Typically, these meet during nap time or designated planning times. They may include some or all teachers. They may be voluntary or required. The intention of the PLC is to foster collaboration among teachers with a shared focus on children. Through PLC, teachers work together to analyze and improve their practice. Focusing PLCs on ECERS encourages teachers to move beyond "What do I need to do?" to "Why is this important for children?"

COACH AND ADMINISTRATOR PARTNERSHIPS

Leadership is recognized as a critical process for changing and improving education. A leader's action or inaction frames the effectiveness of the school. Leaders are instrumental in defining the meaning of school for teachers and parents and thereby affect the nature and quality of the program. Effective coaches work in partnership with the program director or building principal. Coaches and administrators need to work together to effect change. Because of their central role, the director/principal is the gatekeeper to quality.

Coaches who are employed by the center or school district in the role of coach often work directly with teachers. However, the administrator needs to be actively involved, aware of what the coach is doing, and kept informed of progress and needs. The administrator and coach should work in tandem to examine strengths of the program and make plans for tackling subscales and concerns. QRIS coaches, as noted in Chapter 2, are often focused on coaching the director in making program improvements and on coaching the director in coaching her teachers.

ECERS TIPS

These tips were developed based on areas that impact multiple Items as well as those noted as typically lower scoring. Though some Items overlap in the scales, we have created tips for each scale separately. Please refer to Appendix C, "ECERS-3 Materials Checklist," for specifics of the individual Items referred to in the ECERS tips list below.

ECERS-3 TIPS

- Scores are based on observation. There is *no* interview. A classroom is observed for 3 hours. Everything that needs to be seen needs to occur during the 3-hour observation.

- During the 3-hour observation, in order to give a score of 5, the observer is looking for a minimum of 30 minutes of gross motor play with gross motor equipment, either inside or outside. Weather permitting, gross motor play should occur outside. Transition time, where teachers are preparing for the start or aftermath of gross motor time (i.e. putting on outdoor clothing, walking to/from the playground or indoor gym), is *not* considered part of the 30 minutes. Children should go outside every day except when there is active precipitation or health warnings.
- During the 3-hour observation, in order to give a score of 5, the observer is looking for a minimum of 1 hour of free play/access to interest centers and play areas for all children. The minimum 60 minutes of observed time does *not* start until all children are playing and does not include any planning time or completion of prior activity (i.e., washing hands, finishing meals). The time stops as soon as the adult calls for cleanup even if no one starts to clean up. We recommend having over an hour of free play time in the morning to ensure that the minimum of 1 hour is met. If small-group time is incorporated into the free play time, then the time that children are required to participate in the small-group activity is *not* counted as part of the 60 minutes as not *all* children have the opportunity for free play. There are many Items of ECERS-3 that speak to this minimum of 60 minutes. If you don't have the minimum of 60 minutes required, then it affects your score in multiple Items that will not reach a score of 5.
- Play Areas Versus Interest Centers
  - » All interest centers are play areas; all play areas are *not* interest centers.
  - » An interest center is a clearly defined play area for a *particular* type of play. Materials are organized by type and stored so that they are accessible to children. Furniture is provided for the use of materials, if needed. An appropriate amount of space is provided for the type of play being encouraged by materials and the number of children allowed to play in the center. Blocks and dramatic play interest centers are usually larger than other interest centers. All materials in an interest center should relate to the *particular* type of play for that interest center.
  - » A minimum of five interest centers are required for a score of 5 in Item 3 Room Arrangement, including a Cozy Area. The other interest centers can include blocks, dramatic play, fine motor, art, computer, science/nature, library, literacy center, math, and so forth.
  - » For a score of 5, Items 15, 20, 21, and 22, Reading Center/Library, Blocks, Dramatic Play, and Nature/Science are required to meet the definition of an interest center and meet the minimum time requirement of at least 60 minutes.

- Interactions are key. For highest scores, the observer is looking for over 60 specific instances of the varying types of interactions noted in ECERS-3 Indicators. Indicators throughout the scale identify types and the number of times a specific interaction and/or teacher talk/action must be observed.
- There should be *no* waiting time of 3 minutes or longer during any observed transition.
- Read and become familiar with ECERS-3, including the notes for clarification for all Items.

ECERS-R TIPS

- Scores are based on observations and an interview with the classroom teacher for Items that are not observed during the 3-hour observation. ECERS-R provides questions that observers may ask based on information they need to complete scoring the instrument. Teachers should be familiarized with the terms used in the questions so they can honestly answer the observer.
- Any substance labeled "keep out of reach of children" must be kept in a *locked* cabinet.
- Adults and children need to follow handwashing procedures correctly. For Indicators at the 3 level, this means that 75% of children's hands are washed and 75% of adult hands are washed for toileting, 75% for meal times, and 75% of each for all other required times.
- As most observations do not include nap time, teachers should prepare a mat/cot placement chart to show where each is placed in the classroom, and any furniture that is moved. This is particularly useful in classrooms that are smaller or appear crowded.
- Declutter the classroom, ensuring that required materials are accessible to children.
- *Substantial portion of the day* impacts several Items in ECERS-R. Make sure to follow ECERS-R definition and required times based on operating hours for the children. Substantial portion of the day is related to accessibility of materials. The time children spend in a small-group activity may provide them with access to fine motor or art materials, but this is usually not the case for blocks and dramatic play. Ensure all centers are open and accessible during all free choice times to meet substantial portion of the day for all Items required.
- Ensure that the schedule includes at least 1 hour of gross motor time in programs operating 8 or more hours a day. Time is prorated for shorter days. The time may be divided between morning and afternoon.

- There should be *no* waiting time of 3 minutes or longer during any observed transition.
- Read and become familiar with ECERS-R, including the notes for clarification for all Items.

REFLECTION

As coaching uses many approaches, coaching on some areas is often addressed through group meetings, professional learning communities, and/or workshops. Most research on professional development indicates that PD is more effective when there is follow-up through classroom coaching and feedback or technical assistance. This means that simply having a one-shot group event focusing on one subscale or ECERS as a whole, or even several that each focus on individual subscales, is not as effective for making lasting improvements without planned follow-up.

However, ECERS can be used to identify common areas of need across the classrooms, and group discussions and workshops are an appropriate starting place to address common concerns. Through active learning activities, discussions, and communicating ideas among teachers, staff can develop shared understanding of ECERS subscales and Items, and learn new strategies. They also can more deeply understand how children grow and learn, the teacher's role in supporting learning, and the benefits of the recommended practices for children.

Coaches and administrators need to work in partnership to achieve lasting classroom and program improvement. They need to jointly develop goals and plans as well as strategies and responsibilities for affecting change. Working in concert provides less ambiguity for staff as well as ensuring quality is supported and maintained even when there is teacher turnover. In addition to helping administrators become better coaches of teachers, coaches can talk with administrators about how to improve the environment and learning activities, identify resources for workshops, help plan staff activities and meetings to build staff skills, and focus efforts on continuous quality improvement. ECERS Tips are appropriate to share with teachers and staff to provide snapshot guidance on Items often identified as needing modifications.

CHAPTER 12

Last Thoughts and Selected Resources

This final chapter brings us full circle to the purpose of coaching and using ECERS as a framework for program improvement. Specific classroom concerns impacting quality are highlighted, and concerns in coaching are addressed. Also included is a wealth of resources to support coaches and administrators.

IMPROVING QUALITY FOR CHILDREN

ECERS-R and ECERS-3 are about improving the quality of classrooms for children. Coaching is not simply about raising scores. The goal of coaching should be about children having high quality—every day, all day. The focus is on effecting lasting change. It is not about coaching for a one-shot performance for an ECERS assessment. Experts in the field agree that the scales evaluate the "right" things. As a result, either ECERS-R or ECERS-3 is used by most states in their quality rating improvement system (QRIS).

Having moved beyond the obsolete debates on whether early education and child care help or harm development, early childhood educators are focusing on strategies to make child care better. If there is one point on which early childhood educators agree, it is that there is great variety in the quality of early childhood programs and services.

Quality may be most appropriately understood and studied as a blend or configuration of ingredients. ECERS defines quality as specific behaviors observable in the classroom such as teacher sensitivity or involvement, and the presence of structural elements such as materials or schedules. ECERS provides valuable data that can be used to improve classroom practice. Although many factors affect quality, the most important consideration may be the extent to which child-development needs are accounted for in practice. ECERS-R and ECERS-3 are grounded in solid child development and learning theories.

Children learn through play, through active experiences with the materials, through their environment, and through other adults and children.

Child-initiated, child-directed, teacher-supported play is an essential component of developmentally appropriate practice (Bredekamp, 2016). Play comes naturally to young children and serves as a vehicle for them to explore, to experiment, and to make sense of their world. Through play, children build on their experiences—matching the new with the unknown—and enhance their self-esteem—through feeling competent and successful in their activities (Colker & Koralek, 2018). Play is rewarding and has meaning to children. Developmentally appropriate practice is child-centered, recognizing that young children learn through their play and that learning is an ongoing process. In high-quality classrooms, teachers individualize the program for the children to encompass their ages and stages of development and different styles of learning.

ECERS recognizes that play contributes to all types of learning. In high-quality classrooms, teachers serve as designers and facilitators within a room. At best, they create an environment in which children can learn through their play, using the props, materials, and activities available. Teachers support children's learning through interacting with children, asking open-ended questions, and encouraging exploration. These assumptions are in keeping with the Vygotskian notion that more complex cognitive activities develop when there is both a varied and rich environment and teachers who interact with children and enhance children's activities (Berk & Winsler, 1995).

Environments reflect who we are as teachers. ECERS encourages teachers to add new materials to stimulate play; ask children open-ended questions to foster more detailed observations; and take advantage of teachable moments to extend children's learning. Activities and materials that both challenge and encourage each child to grow and learn through direct experience are needed. Professional discourse regarding best practice can deepen teachers' understandings regarding the significance of ECERS as a pedagogical practice and the impact it can have on their children's growth and learning.

The early childhood administrator is widely believed to be one of the keys to providing quality early childhood education. Even highly trained staff are less likely to provide quality in the absence of a director or principal who supports them. The director's actions, efforts, thought processes, purposes, language, and affect impact the teachers' ability to establish and sustain warm, nurturing classroom environments where relationships flourish. When coaches work with teachers, it is imperative that the director or principal be involved.

COMMUNICATION BLOCKS

When coaching efforts to improve classrooms are not effecting change, one of the primary reasons may be communication barriers or blocks. It is often necessary to address blocks head on.

Communication blocks or barriers can take several forms:

- Listening blocks
- Word blocks
- Lack-of-planning blocks
- Seeing-the-need blocks

Listening Blocks

Listening blocks occur when either party is distracted and/or not focused on the interaction. Address this block with a statement such as, "I feel that you may be distracted by something else that's taking away from our conversation. Can you share what is going through your mind right now?" Based on response, it may be necessary to reschedule the conversation or to offer resources to help with the distraction. Sometimes, simply addressing the block removes it and helps to refocus the discussion.

Word Blocks

Word blocks occur when the jargon and/or ECERS specific terms are not understood. For example, a teacher may assume music materials in her classroom are *accessible* to children because if a child asks for one, she opens the cabinet where they are stored. In a case like this, reviewing ECERS definitions for shared meaning is necessary. Discussion around terms such as accessible, interest centers, free play, and engaged can help to provide clarity.

Lack-of-Planning Blocks

A lack-of-planning block occurs when either party is not prepared for the coaching meeting. As a coach, it is imperative that you come to each coaching session with a clear focus and identified outcomes for the session. Beginning the session with a two-way dialogue reviewing the defined goals or tasks agreed upon from the prior session can help to focus the session. Ending each session by establishing agreed-upon goals and tasks to be completed prior to the next session supports this framework. Following up with an email outlining in writing the expectations for the next session and offering resources as relevant may also help.

Seeing-the-Need Blocks

The last communication barrier is what I call the seeing-the-need block. In this situation, the individual being coached doesn't see the need to change or the relevance to his work. On the one hand, this may be because expectations are not clear. In this case, involve the teacher (or director, if coaching the director) in paraphrasing goals, tasks, and improvements needed to ensure shared understanding. On the other hand, the issue may be deeper, involving a lack of shared vision of how children develop and learn and what high quality means. This requires open discussion about the purpose of ECERS, how ECERS impacts quality, and how the purposes align with the program's goals and outcomes for children. Finding common ground is necessary in order to move forward in the best interests of the children.

PUSSYFOOTING AROUND

In an effort to be seen as helpful, nurturing, and flexible, coaches sometimes pussyfoot around any of the previously mentioned blocks. Pussyfooting involves not being frank and honest about your concerns and/or avoiding giving negative feedback. When the coach repeatedly comes to coach and no change has occurred, or agreed-upon tasks are regularly not completed, it becomes necessary to bring the concern to the forefront of the discussion. This isn't about blame or looking for excuses; rather it is about focusing on problem solving. Opening dialogue with sentence starters such as, "I am feeling frustrated because . . ."; "I noticed that when we meet . . ." or "I imagine you may be feeling tired of . . ." can help to begin the dialogue. Not everyone is well suited to being a teacher; nor can everyone be coached to change their dispositions about children and their needs. Counseling individuals out of the field and/or recommending termination or reassignment may be the best course of action.

NO, NO, NEVER, NEVERS

No, No, Never, Nevers are practices that not only represent bad practice but also often result in low scores. If positive outcomes are to be realized for children, the following practices have no place in a high-quality preschool classroom:

- Keeping children in whole group for longer than 15 minutes. Just because they can sit still doesn't mean they should. This practice detracts from more active learning and engagement, and usually reduces the amount of time for free choice and accessibility of materials.
- Using food as a reward or punishment. Food should not be withheld for poor behavior, given as a reward for good behavior, or as a bribe. This creates children with unhealthy relationships with food.

- Using food (e.g., rice, flour, corn meal) as a material in the sand table. This is unhealthy and invites rodents and insects to join your classroom. There are also many who argue against using food for art activities (e.g., finger painting with pudding, using apples as stampers with paint, using food or candy for collage). Not only is this wasteful and spreads germs, but it also encourages children to play with food. Child involvement in making snacks, cooking activities, and tasting activities (e.g., exploring different apples, breads, and spices) is encouraged, as in these activities, food is explored and eaten.
- Discriminating against children by denying access to materials, centers, or activities on the basis of their gender, race, religion, immigration status, language spoken, disability, or family structure. This is contrary to NAEYC's Code of Ethics (2011). For example, both boys and girls should be allowed to engage in dramatic play and in block play. Reasonable accommodations should be provided for children with disabilities to allow access and participation.
- Using the same sponge, cloth, or paper towel for cleaning more than one table or sink. This encourages the spread of germs from one surface to another.
- Adults not washing their own hands. Although teaching staff are getting better at ensuring children wash their hands as required, adults are often not as diligent. Simply wearing gloves does not waive adults washing hands appropriately to prevent the spread of germs.
- Using harsh or severe methods for discipline or classroom management. Adults should not be managing behavior through fear. Severe methods are those that are punitive or associated with hurting children physically or emotionally. Physical methods include the following: hitting, pinching, yanking, or pushing. Other inappropriate methods that have no place in high-quality classrooms include embarrassing, teasing, or belittling a child; yelling or shouting; responding with anger to children; or isolating a child for longer than a couple of minutes, such as in prolonged time-out.
- Leaving children unattended. For their own safety and well-being, children should never be left without adult supervision either inside the classroom or in gross motor spaces. Adults should regularly circulate among children and spaces to ensure children can be seen, heard, and guided, as necessary, as well as to intervene as required to protect children's safety.

COMMON AREAS OF CONCERN IN ECERS-3 AND ECERS-R

- No space for privacy
- Handwashing and sanitation lax or not followed properly
- Safety (major and minor hazards evident)
- Not enough materials (science, blocks, math, art)
- Old books in poor repair
- Not going outside
- Whole group times too long
- Diversity limited to race
- Only one theme in dramatic play
- Substantial portion of the day not met (ECERS-R)
- At least 1 hour of center time (ECERS-3)
- Staff not sitting with children at mealtime
- No limit on computer time for children
- Too much clutter; visual supervision hard
- Too much directed art
- Staff drinking hot coffee and/or eating unhealthy foods in classroom
- Toilets not flushed
- Tables not washed properly
- Too small cubbies for children's coats and clothing so items touch those of another child

---

REFLECTION

ECERS is about raising quality for young children. It's not about "ECERing-up" for a good score for one day. Children deserve high quality each and every day. ECERS is a tool that can be used to support continuous quality improvement. Effective coaches use clear, open communication and feedback and avoid communication blocks. They also don't pussyfoot around by avoiding giving direct feedback and support when needed. Expectations are transparent and in the best interest of children. The "No, No, Never, Nevers" list and "Common Areas of Concern in ECERS-3 and ECERS-R" are appropriate to share with teachers and discuss at staff meetings. Lastly, while a variety of resources are provided to assist coaches in their role, new resources are always being developed. Make sure before using any new resource with staff that it adheres to the intention of ECERS and isn't simply a vehicle to sell a product.

Resources

There are many great books to use with teachers in a book club or PLC. Based on interest, time available, and the demanding lives of adults, it's recommended that the coach or director/principal limit readings to one or two chapters for each discussion.

Some Favorite Books

Bess, C. R. (2010). *The view from the little chair in the corner: Improving teacher practice and early childhood learning.* New York, NY: Teachers College Press.

Christakis, E. (2016). *The importance of being little.* New York, NY: Penguin Books.

Colker, L. J., & Koralek, D. (2018). *High-quality early childhood programs: The what, why, and how.* St. Paul, MN: Redleaf Press.

Cryer, D., Harms, T., & Riley, C. (2003). *All about the ECERS-R.* Raleigh, NC: Pact House Publishing, Kaplan Early Learning Company.

Curtis, D. (2017). *Really seeing children.* Lincoln, NE: Dimensions Educational Research Foundation.

Daly, L., & Beloglovsky, M. (2014). *Loose parts: Inspiring play in young children.* St. Paul, MN: Redleaf Press.

Dombro, A. L., Jablon, J. R., & Stetson, C. (2011). *Powerful interactions: How to connect with children to extend their learning.* Washington, DC: National Association for the Education of Young Children.

Hansel, R. R. (2017). *Creative block play: A comprehensive guide to learning through building.* St. Paul, MN: Redleaf Press.

Isbell, R., & Yoshizawa, S. A. (2016). *Nurturing creativity: An essential mindset for young children's learning.* Washington, DC: National Association for the Education of Young Children.

National Association for the Education of Young Children. (2015). *Expressing creativity in preschool.* Washington, DC: Author.

National Association for the Education of Young Children. (2015). *Exploring math and science in preschool.* Washington, DC: Author.

Strasser, J., & Bresson, L. M. (2017). *Big questions for young minds.* Washington, DC: National Association for the Education of Young Children.

Washington, V. (Ed.). (2017). *Essentials for working with young children* (2nd ed.). Washington, DC: Council for Professional Recognition.

Online Resources on ECERS

The Internet gives access to a plethora of information and materials to support the work of coaches and administrators. Indeed, one can spend hours online combing through websites. A simple search on *ECERS* yields over 350,000 results. Narrowing the search to *ECERS coaching* reduces the results to over 55,000. Here we have narrowed your search by providing a few websites we find to be particularly useful and practical.

1. The Environment Rating Scale Institute (ERSI), www.ersi.info /index.html, provides services related to the use of the family of environmental rating scales. Supplemental materials can be accessed here including playground guidelines, diapering and handwashing procedures, USDA meal guidelines, and table washing procedures. The website should be checked regularly for *Additional Notes* on ECERS-R and ECERS-3. They also provide introductory training on the scales as well as face-to-face training and reliability.
2. Download for free a copy of American Academy of Pediatrics, *Caring for Our Children: National Health and Safety Standards and Guidelines,* cfoc.nrckids.org, for guidance in health and safety issues. In developing ECERS, the authors considered these guidelines in setting the health and safety Items in the scales.
3. Pennsylvania's QRIS webinar of *Overview of ECERS-3,* vimeo .com/124556781, provides a clear introduction to this scale with an exploration of the new Items and Indicators. Though it also includes some Pennsylvania-specific information on their QRIS system and transitioning to ECERS-3, the majority of the 1.5-hour webinar is focused on the scale itself.
4. *Understanding the Meaning of Environment Rating Scale Scores* by ERS authors, www.ersi.info/PDF/Meaning%20of%20 Environment%20Rating%20Scale%20Scores.pdf, provides the authors' stance on scores and their use.
5. Although there are several school supply vendors who have created lists or order forms for materials to meet the materials needed in classrooms based on the supplies and equipment they sell, we have found these resources not linked to vendors to provide detailed checklists for inventory and ordering to be most useful. For ECERS-R, www.simpson.kyschools.us/userfiles/810/ECERS%20 Documents/ECERS-R_Materials_Checklist_Revised%2011-18-13 .pdf, you may find this helpful to use, and for ECERS-3 materials, www.ashland.kyschools.us/userfiles/489/my%20files/ecers-3/ecers -3%20materials%20checklist%20%20revised%2004%2029%20 16.pdf?id=28638.

6. The Bookvine for Children, www.bookvine.com/best-books-to
-align-with-curriculum-and-assessment.html, has put together a
wonderful listing of books to help meet the ECERS categories for
book topics, genres, and selections.

Additional Online Resources

Though not specific to ECERS, here we provide a limited selection of websites to support the work of coaches and administrators through staff development webinars and podcasts, as well as research and blogs.

1. Early Childhood Webinars offers a variety of free webinars. You
can access a list of upcoming webinars as well as prior webinars
from their website (www.earlychildhoodwebinars.com). Topics are
wide-ranging including handling challenging behaviors, nature,
social-emotional development, literacy, play, using loose parts, and
so forth. Webinars are presented by authors and experts in the field.
2. BAM Radio network offers free podcasts and a weekly radio chat
with varied early childhood experts (www.raepica.com/bamradio
-early-childhood-development). You can also access her videos on
Active Learning through YouTube at www.youtube.com/channel
/UC-d20r_dzRuJdQ7J0TEZOMQ.
3. NAEYC hosts webinars several times a year with distinguished
authors of NAEYC books, www.naeyc.org/events/trainings
-webinars/upcoming-webinars, and for NAEYC members, online
discussion groups as well as book discussions can be accessed
through their Hello platform at hello.naeyc.org/home.
4. NAEYC also offers some online training modules (www.naeyc.org
/resources/pd/online-learning). Of specific interest are the modules
on DAP: Focus on Preschool; DAP: Focus on Kindergarten; and
HOT (Higher Order Thinking) Tinkering. The modules are about
1 hour in length, self-paced, and interactive. Cost is $20 per module.
5. ProSolutions Training, www.prosolutionstraining.com/menu, offers
over 100 online courses and modules in early childhood education
and human services. Many are also available in Spanish. They offer
complete CDA (120 hours) and CDA renewal (45 hours) courses.
Also available are 1- to 2-hour modules on topics ranging from
curriculum, child growth and development, health and safety,
classroom management and guidance, cognitive development,
and communications. One-hour modules are quite affordable at
$10 per module. They also offer reasonably priced subscriptions
for individuals and groups with unlimited access for 1 year.
6. Himama, www.himama.com/the-preschool-podcast, provides
weekly podcasts on a wide range of topics for leaders and

teachers. The Preschool Podcasts are free and offer topics presented by professionals in our field including a variety of topics such as challenging behaviors, the importance of play, social-emotional development, staff motivation, and leadership.

7. While there are many who blog about early childhood care and education, with some blogs offering what may be considered highly directed activities and dittos, one of our favorite blogs is *Teach Preschool,* teachpreschool.org/blog, by Deborah J. Stewart, who focuses on learning through play and exploration. Deborah has over 30 years of experience as a director and teacher and owner of a preschool program. She inspires through her commitment to child-led, play-based teaching and learning.

8. Educa developed in New Zealand provides an online platform for centers to support observations, family communication, and staff development. Here we want to highlight their free webinars, www.geteduca.com/webinars, to support leadership and staff development and their blog https://www.geteduca.com/blog/ on early childhood trends.

9. NAEYC's position statement on ethics, www.naeyc.org/sites /default/files/globally-shared/downloads/PDFs/resources /position-statements/Ethics%20Position%20Statement2011 _09202013update.pdf, can be downloaded for free to share with staff and support discussion of the program's beliefs about young children and teachers' roles.

10. Two websites to keep current in national trends and resources are EdWeek's blog on the early years, blogs.edweek.org/edweek /early_years, and National Institute for Early Education Research (NIEER), nieer.org/publications/blog Preschool Matters.

11. At Child Care Exchange, www.childcareexchange.com/eed, you can sign up for their free Exchange Every Day, which offers brief discussions, trends, resources, and/or stories to invite reflection and share information.

12. McCormick Center for Early Childhood Leadership website, mccormickcenter.nl.edu/library, includes a library of selected research and resources focused specifically on leadership.

Coach's Information Form

To help me plan for our coaching session, please complete this form.

Name: Email Address:

Center/School Name:

School Phone: Cell Phone:

Position: # of years in this position:

# of years in the EC field: Previous position(s):

How familiar are you with ECERS?

____ I know it is used to assess preschool classrooms but have never really seen it.

____ I have had an ECERS completed in my classroom(s) and went over the results in depth.

____ I attended an overview session on ECERS.

____ I have a copy of ECERS and have used it on my classroom(s).

What do you feel are three of your strengths in your current position?

1.

2.

3.

What are three areas/things you would like to improve?

1.

2.

3.

What do you hope to gain from working with a coach?

Group or Individual Coaching Questions

Here are some suggested questions to use at group meetings and/or individual coaching sessions to open dialogue and encourage reflection.

1. What excites you most about your job?
2. What happened this week that made you feel successful in your position?
3. What concerns do you have about your classroom?
4. What does an effective teacher (or director) do?
5. What did you enjoy doing as a child?
6. Think about your favorite teacher. What did they do that made them special?
7. As a coach, in what ways can I help you?
8. List feelings and behaviors you associate with the following words: learning, teaching, play, teacher, coaching.
9. What would help you be a better teacher (director) than you already are?
10. What are your strengths as a teacher (director)?
11. What do you think about . . . ?
12. How do you think we can . . . ?
13. What are the key points in the _____ subscale? Why is that important for children? What action steps can you take to improve quality for children in that subscale?
14. What is individualized teaching? What does it look like?
15. Why is free play important in preschool?

ECERS-3 List of Interactions

ECERS-3 includes interactions that require a certain amount of very specific examples in order to give credit. Although over 60 interactions are required throughout the ECERS-3 scale, these are the Indicators that a coach should look and listen for focus her support and feedback, in addition to the Items in the Interaction subscale (Items 28–32).

Item 4. Space for privacy: 7.1
Item 5. Child-related display: 3.3; 5.4
Item 10. Health practices: 3.3; 7.3
Item 12. Helping children expand their vocabulary: 5.2; 7.3
Item 13. Encouraging children to use language: 5.4; 7.1; 7.3
Item 14. Staff use of books with children: 7.1; 7.2; 7.3; 7.4
Item 15. Encouraging children's use of books: 5.2
Item 16. Becoming familiar with print: 3.2; 5.3; 7.2; 7.3; 7.4
Item 17. Fine motor: 5.3; 7.1; 7.3
Item 18. Art: 3.3; 5.3
Item 19. Music and movement: 7.2; 7.3
Item 20. Blocks: 5.5; 7.3
Item 21. Dramatic play: 5.3; 7.3
Item 22. Nature/science: 3.2; 5.2; 5.3; 7.2
Item 23. Math materials and activities: 3.2; 5.2; 7.1; 7.2; 7.3
Item 24. Math in daily events: 3.1; 3.2; 3.3; 5.1; 5.2; 7.1; 7.2; 7.3
Item 25. Understanding written numbers: 3.3; 3.4; 5.3; 7.3; 7.4
Item 26. Promoting acceptance of diversity: 7.1; 7.2
Item 27. Appropriate use of technology: 5.4

Additional Coaching Supports for Interactions

After reviewing the results of a complete ECERS-3 observation, it may be helpful to target shorter observations and feedback sessions on interactions as needed. These short observations may occur during meals, arrival, free play, and/or gross motor time. During these observations, it is helpful to jot down exactly what a teacher or assistant said and/or moments that were missed to support children's learning through adult-child interactions. Here are a few questions to help guide these mini-observations:

- Do staff refer to the displays in their interactions with individual or small groups of children?
- What did staff say to help expand children's vocabulary? Were new words introduced? Explained? Defined?
- What did staff say to support peers talking with one another?
- What questions did staff ask that required more than simply recall or one- or two-word answers?
- What staff-child conversations occurred? What did they talk about?
- What interest centers or play areas did staff show interest in what children were doing? What centers/areas did staff not go to?
- In what ways did staff comment or ask questions to expand children's understanding of language, literacy, and print?
- Did staff use their interactions with children to support children's math knowledge and concepts (one-to-one correspondence, meaning of print number, use of fingers in counting, spatial awareness, shapes in the environment, weight, volume, etc.)?
- In what ways did staff comment or ask questions to support children's understanding of nature/science or concern for the environment?
- In what ways did staff comment or ask questions to support children's reasoning and understanding of relevant concepts?
- What conversation(s) did staff have with a child or group about diversity?
- When did staff join in, but not take over, children's play with materials? What did they say? Talk about?
- Did staff reference current classroom activities or themes in their use of books and interactions with a child or small group of children?

ECERS-3 Materials Checklist

The materials listed are some examples of what you might see in various learning centers; all examples listed do not have to be present to give credit. Coaches, teachers, and administrators can use this as a checklist to see where additional materials are needed.

15. Encouraging Children's Use of Books

3.1 At least 15 books.
5.1 Many books: at least 20 books for 10 children, or 30 books for 15 children plus 1 more for each additional child. Calculate based on the highest number of children attending at any time.
7.1 Books reflective of current classroom theme = five books.

Possible Topics

☐ Differing abilities   ☐ Health   ☐ Nature/science
☐ Different cultures   ☐ Jobs/work   ☐ People
☐ Different races   ☐ Males and females   ☐ Sports/hobbies
☐ Feelings   ☐ Math

17. Fine Motor

3.1 Total of 10 choices.
5.1 All categories must be represented, at least one type from each category.
7.2 Containers and/or accessible storage shelves have labels to encourage self-help.

Interlocking Building Materials

☐ Bristle blocks   ☐ Legos   ☐ Tinker toys
☐ Duplos   ☐ Lincoln Logs   ☐ Other (list)

Art Materials

☐ Crayons   ☐ Playdough   ☐ Other (list)
☐ Markers   ☐ Scissors
☐ Pencils   ☐ Hole punches

Puzzles

- ☐ Floor puzzles
- ☐ Frame puzzles
- ☐ Knobbed puzzles
- ☐ Other (list)
- ☐ Diversity reflected in puzzles/fine motor materials

Manipulatives

- ☐ Gears
- ☐ Links
- ☐ Mr. Potato Head
- ☐ Nuts and bolts
- ☐ Pattern blocks
- ☐ Pegs with peg boards
- ☐ Pop beads
- ☐ Sewing cards
- ☐ Snap blocks
- ☐ Stringing beads
- ☐ Table blocks
- ☐ Train tracks
- ☐ Unifix cubes
- ☐ Zip, snap, button toys/vests
- ☐ Other (list)

---

18. Art

*All materials must be accompanied by paper, as needed, or another surface for use when carrying out artwork.

5.1 At least one material from each category. Note to support diversity: race/culture reflected in art materials.

Drawing

- ☐ Chalk
- ☐ Chalkboards
- ☐ Crayons
- ☐ Dry erase boards
- ☐ Markers

Paints

- ☐ Finger paints
- ☐ Tempera paints
- ☐ Watercolors
- ☐ Other (list)

3D

- ☐ Boxes
- ☐ Clay
- ☐ Modeling compound
- ☐ Pipe cleaners
- ☐ Playdough
- ☐ Wood scraps
- ☐ "Junk" (e.g., cardboard tubes and packing material)
- ☐ Other (list)

Collage

- ☐ Feathers
- ☐ Felt scraps
- ☐ Glitter
- ☐ Magazines
- ☐ Paper scraps
- ☐ Paste
- ☐ Pom-poms
- ☐ Sequins
- ☐ Yarn/string
- ☐ Buttons
- ☐ Cardboard tubes
- ☐ Cotton balls
- ☐ Egg cartons
- ☐ Other (list)

Tools

- ☐ Hole punches
- ☐ Playdough tools
- ☐ Rollers
- ☐ Ruler
- ☐ Scissors

- ☐ Sponge painters
- ☐ Stamps/stamp pad
- ☐ Stapler
- ☐ Stencils
- ☐ Tape

- ☐ Dot markers
- ☐ Brushes
- ☐ Other (list)

---

19. Music and Movement

3.1   At least three music materials.

5.1   At least 10 instruments or if used in group time, at least 1 per child participating. Credit is not given if all materials are of the same type.

3.1, 5.1   Recorded music (played by staff or children) may count for one music material.

Instruments

- ☐ Bells
- ☐ Castanets
- ☐ Cymbals
- ☐ Drums
- ☐ Electric keyboard
- ☐ Hardwood blocks with mallet

- ☐ Maracas
- ☐ Piano
- ☐ Rain stick
- ☐ Rhythm sticks
- ☐ Triangles
- ☐ Shakers
- ☐ Tambourine

- ☐ Wrist bells
- ☐ Xylophones
- ☐ Instruments/music that reflect diverse cultures
- ☐ Other (list)

---

20. Blocks

*Interlocking blocks (e.g., Legos) or blocks with most sides less than 2 inches do *not* count as blocks.

3.1, 3.2   Enough space, blocks, and accessories for two children to build sizable independent structures at the same time.

5.1   Enough space, blocks, and accessories (three types) for three children to build sizable independent structures at the same time.

5.2   Block shelves labeled. Accessory bins *and* shelves labeled.

7.1   Requires large hollow blocks.

Blocks

Unit Blocks
- ☐ Wood
- ☐ Foam
- ☐ Plastic

Large Hollow Blocks
- ☐ Wood
- ☐ Cardboard
- ☐ Plastic

Block Accessories

☐ Animals
☐ Small people
☐ Vehicles

☐ Other (road signs, fences, trees, small buildings, etc.) (list)

**Accessories should enhance, rather than detract, from block play. If use of vehicles or other toys interferes with building, credit is not given.

Other Materials in Block Center

**NOTE: Space for block play must not be used for other purposes that interfere with the use of blocks.

☐ Diversity
☐ Race
☐ Culture

☐ Age
☐ Differing abilities
☐ Nontraditional gender roles

---

21. Dramatic Play

*Small pretend play materials found in block or fine motor areas do not count in scoring this Item.

3.1 Some materials for children to act out family roles themselves.
5.1 Many and varied materials, including dolls, child-sized furniture, play foods, cooking/eating utensils, dress-up clothes for boys and girls plus additional materials or theme.
7.1 At least four clear examples of materials to represent diversity.

Theme: Housekeeping

Required:
☐ Child-sized furniture (stove, washer/dryer, etc.)
☐ Cooking/eating utensils
☐ Dolls
☐ Dress-up clothes for both boys and girls
☐ Play food

Additional housekeeping materials:
☐ Doll clothes
☐ Doll furniture (bed, high chair, stroller, etc.)
☐ Mirror
☐ Stuffed animals
☐ Telephone
☐ Other (list)

Theme: Different Kinds of Work

☐ Construction (hats, shovels, tools, etc.)
☐ Farmer/gardener (rakes, shovels, seed packets, pumpkins, etc.)

☐ Firefighter (hose, uniform, buckets, helmet, boots, etc.)
☐ Medical (gauze bandages, doctor's kit, dolls, etc.)

- [ ] Office play (office supplies, desk, briefcase, etc.)
- [ ] Post office (mailbox, envelopes, postcards, mailbag, jacket, hat, etc.)
- [ ] Restaurant (tables and chairs, menus, play money, aprons, etc.)
- [ ] Store (cash register, play food, empty food cartons, bags, pretend money, etc.)
- [ ] Zoo keeper/vet (stuffed or other toy animals, tickets, money, etc.)
- [ ] Other

Theme: Fantasy

- [ ] Costumes, including hats, capes, fancy dress-ups, crown, etc.
- [ ] Magic wands or other accessories
- [ ] Simple, nonfrightening masks or face paint
- [ ] Things to act out familiar stories
- [ ] Other (list)

Theme: Leisure

- [ ] Boating
- [ ] Camping
- [ ] Fishing
- [ ] Parties
- [ ] Picnic
- [ ] Sports
- [ ] Vacation
- [ ] Other

Dramatic Play Materials That Reflect Diversity

- [ ] Cultural cooking utensils (e.g., wok)
- [ ] Dolls (different races, cultures)
- [ ] Equipment used by people with disabilities
- [ ] Menus
- [ ] Multicultural dress-up clothes
- [ ] Pretend foods of different cultures
- [ ] Other (list)

22. Nature/Science

*Materials must be in Science Interest Center to receive credit!

3.1 At least five nature/science materials from two categories.
3.3 Sand or water with appropriate toys accessible.
5.1 At least 15 materials with some from each of the five categories, *including at least five nature/science books*. Sand/water can be counted as 1 of the 15 materials.
7.2 Requires one or more pets/plants that children can observe, help care for, and that are talked about with children.

Living Things Children Can Observe Closely or Care For

- [ ] Ant farm
- [ ] Aquarium with fish, snails, or other animals
- [ ] Butterfly hatching kit
- [ ] Class pet
- [ ] Eggs that hatch
- [ ] Plants
- [ ] Window bird feeder
- [ ] Worm farm
- [ ] Other (list)

Natural Objects

- ☐ Birds' nest
- ☐ Collections of seeds
- ☐ Different types of wood
- ☐ Insects in transparent plastic
- ☐ Leaves
- ☐ Nuts
- ☐ Pinecones
- ☐ Rocks
- ☐ Seashells
- ☐ Other (list)

**Note: Plastic bugs and dinosaurs are not considered science materials.

Factual Books/Nature-Science Picture Games

- ☐ Books (five count as one item)
- ☐ Science-themed board games
- ☐ Matching game (e.g., body parts)
- ☐ Puzzles with nature pictures or natural sequences
- ☐ Matching texture boards
- ☐ Smelling cans with different things (to match or sort)
- ☐ Other (list)

Nature/Science Tools

- ☐ Binoculars/viewers
- ☐ Balance scales *with natural objects to weigh*
- ☐ Color paddles
- ☐ Kaleidoscope
- ☐ Lifting objects with levers/ pulleys
- ☐ Magnets *with magnetic/ nonmagnetic things*
- ☐ Magnifying glasses
- ☐ Microscope *and slides to look at*
- ☐ Prisms
- ☐ Sensory bottles (oil and water, etc.)
- ☐ Tornado tubes
- ☐ Using a rain gauge to record how much rain fell
- ☐ Other (list)

Sand or Water with Toys (Indoors or Outdoors)

- ☐ Buckets
- ☐ Funnels
- ☐ Measuring cups/ spoons
- ☐ Pails
- ☐ Rakes
- ☐ Sand molds
- ☐ Scoops
- ☐ Shovels
- ☐ Sifters/sieve
- ☐ Spray bottles
- ☐ Turkey baster
- ☐ Trowels
- ☐ Unbreakable containers (e.g., plastic bowls)
- ☐ Other (list)

**Note: Sand/water tables do not need to be in the Science Center; if stand-alone, this can be an additional interest center providing appropriate materials and storage are available.

---

23. Math Materials and Activities

*Credit not given for posters, books, and other displayed materials nor play materials with written numbers.
**A material may only be counted in one category.

3.1   At least two materials from each of the three categories.
5.1   At least 10 materials total, with at least 3 from each category.
7.1   Math materials/activities related to current topics of interest included.

Counting/Comparing Quantities

☐ Abacus
☐ Chart and graph activities for children to use by placing materials into cells
☐ Dice/dominoes
☐ Five/ten frame cards
☐ Games that require children to figure out more or less
☐ Games with dice
☐ Pegboards with numbers printed and holes to match
☐ Playing cards
☐ Puzzles where written numbers are matched to quantities
☐ Small objects *to count into numbered containers*
☐ Unifix cubes
☐ Other (list)

Measuring/Comparing Sizes and Parts of Whole (Fractions)

☐ Balance scale *with things to weigh*
☐ Bathroom scale
☐ Games where halves are matched to the whole (fractions)
☐ Games with parts to divide and put back together to make the whole
☐ Height chart *if regularly used to measure children's growth*
☐ Math links
☐ Measuring cups and spoons *with materials to measure*
☐ Nested cups
☐ Puzzles with geometric shapes
☐ Graduated puzzles
☐ Rulers, yardsticks, tape measures
☐ Shapes-matching games where geometric shapes are divided into parts (fractions)
☐ Thermometer
☐ Other (list)

Familiarity with Shapes

☐ 3D shapes
☐ Attribute blocks of different sizes, shapes, colors
☐ Geoboards (boards with pegs to which rubber bands are attached to make shapes)
☐ Magnetic shapes
☐ Parquetry blocks with patterns
☐ Puzzles with different geometric shapes
☐ Shape sorters
☐ Shape stencils
☐ Unit blocks with image/outline labels on shelves
☐ Other (list)

---

25. Understanding Written Numbers

3.1   Some print numbers in display materials.
5.1   At least three different play materials that help show children meaning of print numbers.

Print Numbers in Display Materials

*Must have pictures that show what the number means.

- ☐ Signs for number of children allowed in center *with stick figures/object to represent the number*
- ☐ Poster with numbers and corresponding image showing that number of objects

- ☐ Attendance charts (showing stick figures/photos identifying children present/absent and numerals)
- ☐ Class-made charts and graphs
- ☐ Other (list)

Play Materials with Numbers

- ☐ Calculator
- ☐ Cards
- ☐ Cash register
- ☐ Counting books
- ☐ Dice/dominoes
- ☐ Grocery receipts/grocery store ads/fliers
- ☐ Magnetic numbers

- ☐ Menu with prices
- ☐ Number lacing cards
- ☐ Number puzzles
- ☐ Number stamps/paint sponges
- ☐ Spinners
- ☐ Telephones
- ☐ Toy clock

Play Materials Showing Meaning of Print Numbers

- ☐ Matching picture/number cards
- ☐ Pegboards with numbers printed and holes to match
- ☐ Playing cards
- ☐ Puzzle with numbered fingers on one hand

- ☐ Puzzles with number on one piece and that number of dots on matching piece
- ☐ Simple number card games
- ☐ Other (list)

---

26. Promoting Acceptance of Diversity

*Materials must be easily visible for credit. Books should be easy to find by looking at book covers.

NOTE: See p. 64 in ECERS-3 scale: One example consists of a contrast in diversity. Examples may be found in one Item (such as a picture of children showing a child with a disability and one without) or two separate Items stored close together (such as two dolls of different races in the dramatic play area or small people of different ages in the block center).

3.1   At least three examples of racial/cultural diversity in materials.
5.1   At least two different types of dramatic play props representing different races or cultures.

5.2   At least 10 positive examples of diversity with at least 1 example each of books, displayed pictures, and play materials. *Materials may be counted in either 5.1 *or* 5.2, but not both.

5.3   Classroom materials include at least four of the five types of diversity.

Books

*Examples should be easy to find by looking at book covers.

☐ Race   ☐ Age   ☐ Nontraditional
☐ Culture   ☐ Differing abilities   gender role

Displayed Pictures

*Do not count pictures of children and their families.

☐ Race   ☐ Age   ☐ Nontraditional
☐ Culture   ☐ Differing abilities   gender role

Play Materials

*Examples: dolls, puppets, play food, cultural cooking utensils, small people figurines, wheelchair for dolls, musical instruments from various cultures, puzzles

☐ Race   ☐ Age   ☐ Nontraditional
☐ Culture   ☐ Differing abilities   gender role

Determining Major and Minor Hazards

According to the ECERS-3, "a major safety hazard is one where the risk of serious injury is very high. A minor hazard is either one where the consequences would not be as great, or the accident would be less likely, due for example to the nature of the supervision, the characteristics of the children in the group, or the amount of exposure to the hazard. It is important when noting hazards, not to imagine every possible accident. Instead focus on the seriousness of the hazard and how likely is it to happen" (p. 34).

Examples of Indoor and Outdoor Major/Minor Hazards

When determining whether to weigh a hazard as a major or minor, a helpful hint is to ask yourself if the outcome of a potentially risky situation or a child's encounter with this particular object would require immediate and serious medical attention and the likelihood of this happening based on teacher supervision and children's accessibility. If supervision is adequate, the risk of something happening is less likely (i.e., a teacher standing nearby areas of items that could cause a potential accident, like a large air-conditioning unit jutting out of the building in the outdoor gross motor space in order to prevent children from getting too close to it).

(Please note: This is not meant to be an exhaustive checklist of all potential hazards but examples of ones that observers have seen while conducting recent observations and things to look out for.)

- Uncovered electric outlets next to water table, sink, or any place near running water.
- Cleaning solutions/chemicals unlocked and within reach of children.
- Plug-in air fresheners at children's level.
- Lightbulbs in any areas used by the children should have a protective surfacing to prevent injury of glass should it shatter or break.
- Unsecured cords from blinds or shades posing a potential risk of choking should be tied up and away from children's reach.

- Temperature on outdoor playground equipment (rubber or metal pieces of equipment can become too hot to touch with warmer temperatures).
- Loose, unraveling basketball nets as an entrapment hazard.
- Street distance and no bollards within 30 feet of streets or parking lots.
- Large, open gaps on and/or under fencing pose a potential risk of children being able to leave area or trap body parts.
- Debris on the playground (i.e., cigarette butts, glass bottles).
- Large air-conditioning units in gross motor space(s) jutting out that are on children's level and can pose a potential threat of children running into and injuring themselves on them.
- Inappropriate child-sized playground equipment for age group (refer to Playground Safety Sheet for accurate measurements).
- No safety guards, like screens or bars outside of open windows in classrooms located above first floor.
- No railing on stairways for children to use when holding on when going up and down the stairs.
- Hot beverages left around children and at their level.
- Large, heavy items that children pull down on shelving that is not anchored or is top-heavy (i.e., televisions, computers, CD players).
- Medications not locked up and accessible to children.
- Knives or other sharp items (large scissors, box cutters, tape dispensers).
- Open or unlocked doors accessible to children leading to large staircases, boiler rooms, or other unsafe areas.
- Anything labeled "Keep out of reach of children" that is accessible to children.
- Toxic plants around playground.
- Uncapped bolts on playground perimeter.
- Loose-wired fencing.
- Metal prongs on fencing.
- Uncovered outlets.
- Use of thumbtacks in the classroom.
- Loose floor tiles.
- Cleaning solutions/chemicals unlocked but stored high up and away from children's reach.
- Protective surfacing but not enough in a fall zone for equipment up to 60 inches high.

Developed by staff at the NJ Center for Quality Ratings, 2016.

References

American Academy of Pediatrics, American Public Health Association, National Resource Center for Health and Safety in Child Care and Early Education. (2011). *Caring for our children: National health and safety performance standards; Guidelines for Early Care and Education Programs* (3rd ed.). Elk Grove Village, IL: American Academy of Pediatrics. Retrieved from cfoc.nrckids.org

Barnett, W. S. (2011). Effectiveness of early educational intervention. *Science, 333,* 975–978.

Berk, L. E., & Winsler, A. (1995). *Scaffolding children's learning: Vygotsky and early childhood education.* Washington, DC: National Association for the Education of Young Children.

Bohart, H., Charner, K., & Koralek, D. (2015). *Spotlight on young children: Exploring play.* Washington, DC: National Association for the Education of Young Children.

Bredekamp, S. (2016). *Effective practice in early childhood education* (3rd ed.). Boston, MA: Pearson.

Caffarella, R. S., & Barnett, B. B. (1994). Characteristics of adult learners and foundations of experiential learning. *New Directions for Adult and Continuing Education, 1994*(62), 29–42. doi:10.1002/ace.36719946205

Camilli, G., Vargas, S., Ryan, S., & Barnett, W. S. (2010). Meta-analysis of the effects of early education interventions on cognitive and social development. *Teachers College Record, 112*(3), 579–620.

Charlesworth, R. (2015). *Math and science for young children* (8th ed.). Boston, MA: Pearson.

Christakis, E. (2016). *The importance of being little.* New York, NY: Penguin Books.

Colker, L. J., & Koralek, D. (2018). *High-quality early childhood programs: The what, why, and how.* St. Paul, MN: Redleaf Press.

Collins, M. F. (2014). Preschool: Sagacious, sophisticated, and sedulous: The importance of discussing 50-cent words with preschoolers. In A. Schillady (Ed.), *Spotlight on young children: Exploring language and literacy* (pp. 14–21). Washington, DC: National Association for the Education of Young Children.

Copple, C., Bredekamp, S., Koralek, D., & Charner, K. (Eds.). (2013). *Developmentally appropriate practice: Focus on preschoolers.* Washington, DC: National Association for the Education of Young Children.

Cryer, D., Harms, T., & Riley, C. (2003). *All about the ECERS-R.* Raleigh, NC: Pact House Publishing, Kaplan Early Learning Company.

Curtis, D. (2017). *Really seeing children.* Lincoln, NE: Dimensions Educational Research Foundation.

Curtis, D., & Carter, M. (2015). *Designs for living and learning: Transforming early childhood environments* (2nd ed.). St. Paul, MN: Redleaf Press.

Curtis, D., Lebo, D., Cividanes, W. C. M., & Carter, M. (2013). *Reflecting in communities of practice: A workbook for early childhood educators.* St. Paul, MN: Redleaf Press.

Daly, L., & Beloglovsky, M. (2014). *Loose parts: Inspiring play in young children.* St. Paul, MN: Redleaf Press.

Dombro, A. L., Jablon, J. R., & Stetson, C. (2011). *Powerful interactions: How to connect with children to extend their learning.* Washington, DC: National Association for the Education of Young Children.

Elias, M. J., Zins, J. E., Graczyk, P. A., & Weissberg, R. P. (2003). Implementation, sustainability, and scaling up of social–emotional and academic innovations in public schools. *School Psychology Review, 32,* 303–319.

Englehart, D., Mitchell, D., Albers-Biddle, J., Jennings-Towle, K., & Forestieri, M. (2016). *STEM play: Integrating inquiry into learning centers.* Lewisville, NC: Gryphon House.

Epstein, A. S. (2014). *The intentional teacher: Choosing the best strategies for young children's learning.* Washington, DC: National Association for the Education of Young Children.

Erikson Institute, Early Math Collaborative. (2014). *Big ideas of early mathematics: What teachers of young children need to know.* Boston, MA: Pearson.

Hamre, B., Hatfield, B., Pianta, R., & Jamil, F. (2013). Evidence for general and domain-specific elements of teacher-child interactions: Associations with preschool children's development. *Child Development, 85*(3), 1257–1274. doi:10.1111/cdev.12184

Hansel, R. R. (2017). *Creative block play: A comprehensive guide to learning through building.* St. Paul, MN: Redleaf Press.

Harms, T., Clifford, R. M., & Cryer, D. (2005). *Early childhood environment rating scale* (rev. ed.). New York, NY: Teachers College Press.

Harms, T., Clifford, R. M., & Cryer, D. (2015). *Early childhood environment rating scale* (3rd ed.). New York, NY: Teachers College Press.

Isbell, R., & Yoshizawa, S. A. (2016). *Nurturing creativity: An essential mindset for young children's learning.* Washington, DC: National Association for the Education of Young Children.

Jablon, J. R., Dombro, A. L., & Johnsen, S. (2016). *Coaching with powerful interactions: A guide to partnering with early childhood teachers.* Washington, DC: National Association for the Education of Young Children.

Katz, L. (1972). Developmental stages of preschool teachers. *Elementary School Journal, 73*(1), 50–54.

Kostelnik, M. J., Soderman, A. K., Whiren, A. P., & Rupiper, M. L. (2015). *Developmentally appropriate curriculum: Best practices in early childhood education* (6th ed.). Upper Saddle River, NJ: Pearson.

National Association for the Education of Young Children. (2011). *NAEYC code of ethical conduct and statement of commitment.* Washington, DC: Author.

National Association for the Education of Young Children. (2009). Developmentally appropriate practice in early childhood programs serving children from birth through age 8. Retrieved from www.naeyc.org/sites/default/files/globally-shared/downloads/PDFs/resources/position-statements/PSDAP.pdf

National Early Literacy Panel. (2008). *Developing early literacy: Report of the National Early Literacy Panel.* Executive summary. Washington, DC: National Institute for Literacy.

Schickedanz, J. A., & Collins, M. F. (2013). *So much more than the ABCs: The early phases of reading and writing.* Washington, DC: National Association for the Education of Young Children.

Seplocha, H. (2017). Using high level questions during read alouds. In J. Strasser & L. M. Bresson, *Big questions for young minds: Extending children's thinking* (pp. 57–62). Washington, DC: National Association for the Education of Young Children.

Seplocha, H., & Strasser, J. (2009). Using fanciful magical language in preschool. *Teaching Young Children, 2*(4), 17–19.

Shonkoff, J. P. (2017). Breakthrough impacts: What science tells us about supporting early childhood development? *Young Children, 72*(2), 8–16.

Strasser, J., & Bresson, L. M. (2017). *Big questions for young minds.* Washington, DC: National Association for the Education of Young Children.

Tomlinson, H., & Hyson, M. (2012). Cognitive development in the preschool years. In C. Copple (Ed.), *Growing minds: Building strong cognitive foundations in early childhood* (pp. 33–40). Washington, DC: National Association for the Education of Young Children.

Washington, V. (Ed.). (2017). *Essentials for working with young children* (2nd ed.). Washington, DC: Council for Professional Recognition.

Whitebook, M., McLean, C., & Austin, L. J. E. (2016). *Early Childhood Workforce Index—2016.* Berkeley, CA: Center for the Study of Child Care Employment, University of California, Berkeley.

Index

Page numbers followed by *f* indicate figures.

About the Author

Holly Seplocha, EdD, has worked for more than 40 years as a teacher, administrator, university professor, teacher educator, consultant, researcher, presenter, and advocate for children and families. She is a professor of early childhood education at William Paterson University in New Jersey and teaches graduate courses in literacy and language development, early childhood learning environments and assessment, and research. Holly is a recognized leader in the early childhood community and has made hundreds of presentations for teachers, parents, and administrators locally, nationally, and abroad. She has authored a variety of articles on leadership, diversity, parent involvement, literacy, and technology. Holly is highly reliable and has completed hundreds of classroom observations using ECERS-3 and ECERS-R, trained and brought others to reliability, and worked with countless teachers, coaches, and administrators to improve the quality of their early childhood programs.

Holly is also the project director of the NJ Center for Quality Ratings housed at WPU, working with the New Jersey Department of Education to design and implement a system for rating the quality of preschool programs across the state. She recently completed a video series for the NJDOE for use in teacher training on the NJ Preschool Classroom Teaching Guidelines, which she also developed for NJDOE. She was also the project director of the Early Learning Improvement Consortium, working with the NJDOE to develop, implement, and train trainers in an authentic assessment system for literacy linked to New Jersey preschool and kindergarten standards, and to conduct statewide evaluations of preschool and kindergarten classrooms using ECERS.

Holly is a former National Early Childhood Teacher Educator of the Year and was named one of 125 Distinguished Alumni of Wheelock College for their 125th-year anniversary. She is an active member of NAEYC, serving as a consulting editor for *Young Children,* and regularly as a featured presenter at NAEYC conferences. Holly willingly shares her knowledge, her passion, her wit, and her optimism. She is a lively and engaging presenter and writer whose goal is to impact classroom practice and children's learning by scaffolding directors, supervisors, coaches, teachers, and parents to grow and reflect, as they explore *best practices* for young children.